TWAYNE'S WORLD AUTHORS SERIES
A Survey of the World's Literature

FRANCE

Maxwell A. Smith, Guerry Professor of French, Emeritus
The University of Chattanooga
Former Visiting Professor in Modern Languages
The Florida State University
EDITOR

Choderlos de Laclos

TWAS 502

Choderlos de Laclos

D'après un pastel appartenant à Mme Louis de Chauvigny.

CHODERLOS
DE LACLOS

By RONALD C. ROSBOTTOM
Ohio State University

TWAYNE PUBLISHERS
A DIVISION OF G. K. HALL & CO., BOSTON

Published in 1978 by Twayne Publishers,
A Division of G. K. Hall & Co.
All Rights Reserved

Printed on permanent/durable acid-free paper and bound
in the United States of America

First Printing

Library of Congress Cataloging in Publication Data

Rosbottom, Ronald C., 1942–
Choderlos de Laclos.

(Twayne's world authors series ; TWAS 502 : France)
Bibliography: p. 157–161
Includes index.
1. Laclos, Pierre Ambroise François Choderlos de, 1741–1803.
Les liaisons dangereuses.
PO1993.L22L68   843'.6   78–18722
ISBN 0-8057-6343-0

FOR MICHAEL
whose love and
laughs sustain me

Contents

About the Author

Ronald C. Rosbottom was born in New Orleans in 1942, and received his B.A. from Tulane University and his M.A. and Ph.D. from Princeton University. A member of the Department of Romance Languages and Literatures at Ohio State University, Professor Rosbottom is Executive Secretary of the American Society for Eighteenth-Century Studies. He is as well editorial advisor to *Eighteenth-Century Studies* and to *The Eighteenth Century: A Journal of Theory and Interpretation* (formerly *Studies in Burke and His Time*). Professor Rosbottom is author of *Marivaux's Novels: Theme and Function in Erly Eighteenth-Century Narrative,* editor of volumes five and six of *Studies in Eighteenth-Century Culture,* and has written numerous articles on various aspects of eighteenth-century French literature and critical theory.

Preface

Readers skim prefaces, if they read them at all. What is it about prefaces that make them so easily and often ignored? Even worse, if read, they are distrusted. Of course, they almost always have a justificatory tone about them; they are a means of protection for the author chary of unfriendly reviewers ("Don't blame me for not writing about that; I specifically said I wasn't in my preface"). And, they are essentially dishonest, or misleading at best. Most prefaces (from the Latin *praefātio,* "a saying beforehand"), this one included, are written *after* the fact; they tend to explain how the book they introduce became different from the book the author set out to write. Laclos was aware of the ambiguous nature of prefatory essays and used this knowledge with ironic success in the two fictitious prefaces to *Les Liaisons dangereuses*. My purpose is different in this preface, though probably just as suspect.

As bespeaks the nature of the series in which this study appears, this book is meant first to be an introduction and companion for the reader who cannot or has not read *Les Liaisons dangereuses* in French. However, and I hasten to add this point, this study was written with those in mind as well who can and have read Laclos's novel in the language in which it was written. The study is organized around the assumption, disconcerting at first, but soon seen as being natural, that the novel must be read at least *twice* (not a small task for a four-hundred-page book). Ideally, I would ask my readers to read chapters 1–3 of my study first, then to read *Les Liaisons dangereuses,* then chapters 4–6, and finally to reread the *Liaisons*. Laclos's masterwork deserves no less attention, and the persistent reader's rewards will be surpassed only by those of the rereader.

Chapter 1 of this monograph is biographical. It chronicles the life of Laclos, placing appropriate emphasis on those works of his that defined his attempts to obtain citizenship in the republic of letters. Chapter 2 concerns the publication, reception, and nature of his only novel. It provides the uninitiated reader with just enough information on the novel's story, characters, and contexts to facilitate a sufficient first reading. It avoids any "interpretations" that might interfere with that reading. For instance, I have abstained, as much as possible, from addressing some of the commonplaces of Laclos criticism, such as the question of Manichaeanism, the Don Juan myth, the "pre-Revolutionary" aspects of this dangerous novel, and so forth. Chapter 3 is an introduction to the themes and rhetoric of the narrative subgenre of which the *Liaisons* is perhaps the prime example: the letter novel. Chapters 4–6 are more hermeneutic in nature, though again my concern was to provide potential strategies for reading the novel without suggesting that any of them are necessarily essential to its final comprehension. Chapter 4 examines the problematics and thematics of reading and writing in the novel, as well as how the traditional ways of assigning meaning to such a text often prove insufficient. Chapter 5 examines the dominant relationship of the novel, that of Merteuil and Valmont, using a critical model that takes into account the communicational aspects of letter fiction. Chapter 6, in the guise of a conclusion, offers a perspective on Laclos's work that might help to explain its bizarre history and reputation.

Les Liaisons dangereuses is not a text to which it is easy to assign meaning, though it has attracted such efforts for almost two hundred years. In fact, writing a book on Laclos and his novel is a deceptive task. On one level, it would seem relatively simple. *Les Liaisons dangereuses* is a lengthy work, to be sure, but none of its essential narrative structures (themes, plot, characterization) is obscure or unduly complex. The author's life, though not well-documented, is relatively straightforward, despite a confusing period during the Revolution. And to aid the writer of such a study, there is an impressive bibliography of secondary sources dating from the early nineteenth century. Yet this is where the task of introducing Laclos becomes complex; the commentary, especially on his novel, is immense, contradictory, often brilliant, more often repetitious, and inclusive of just about every facet of the novel. This sense of trepidation definitely increases after one reads two works: Jean-Luc Seylaz's *"Les Liaisons dangereuses" et la création romanesque chez Laclos* and Laurent Versini's *Laclos et la tradition: Essai sur les sources et la technique des "Liaisons dangereuses."* Seylaz's work is one of the best and most original examples of traditional literary scholarship available in French, and Versini's book is a monument to literary history: all one ever wanted to know and had not even thought of asking about novelistic themes and procedures before 1789. Besides these two relatively recent studies, every type of critic, from Paul Hazard and Daniel Mornet to Roland Barthes and Tzvetan Todorov, has tried to understand and make understandable *Les Liaisons dangereuses.*

However — and this is (as my reader has been anticipating) the reason for the present effort — this fascinating novel still has a relatively limited audience, almost entirely Francophone. Such a situation was not caused by a lack of good translations: two quite serviceable ones are still available in English (see the Selected Bibliography for details). The reasons lie elsewhere. Laclos is not a well-known name even to those who have some knowledge of French culture. He was not a member, nor even an enemy, of the group of *philosophes* that included Voltaire and Diderot; in many ways he was eclipsed as a novelist by the generations that followed him, those of Balzac, Flaubert, and Proust, as well as by the uniqueness of his contemporary, Sade. Being an epistolary novelist, and a citizen of the ancien régime, Laclos quickly was covered with the mantle of anachronism. Ignored by such Francophiles as Henry James, who gave international prestige to a whole generation of French writers, he remains an unknown quantity to Anglo-American readers and critics. So, despite the extensive documentation and interpretation of Laclos in French, there is still relatively little pertinent material available on the author or his novel in English.

The emphasis of this study will then be twofold: to spread the word about this unjustly neglected writer and his novel, and to provide a number of possible strategies for reading the *Liaisons*. My study cannot be called definitive; it is a place to begin, and perhaps an enticement to begin. My hope is that what I have to say and to infer will make *Les Liaisons dangereuses* a better-known work, in this country and in other English-speaking cultures. It deserves more attention; it demands patience, but I believe the effort expended will be considered worthwhile.

RONALD C. ROSBOTTOM

Columbus, Ohio

Acknowledgments

This is an appropriate opportunity to thank those academic units of The Ohio State University — The Graduate School, the College of Humanities, and the Department of Romance Languages and Literatures — which provided me with the funds, the released time, and the amenities for the preparation of this study. I am very grateful for these various expressions of confidence. I trust this book will be worthy of them.

I would like to thank Lloyd Free, editor of *Laclos: Critical Approaches to "Les Liaisons dangereuses"* (Madrid: Porrúa, 1978), for allowing me to use a version of an essay which appeared in that collection, "Dangerous Connections: A Communicational Approach to *Les Liaisons dangereuses*," in Chapter 5 of the present study.

My gratitude as well goes to John Erickson, editor of the journal *L'Esprit Créateur,* for permitting the use in Chapter 3 of a longer version of an essay that appears in a special number on epistolary fiction: "Motifs in Epistolary Fiction: Analysis of a Narrative Subgenre," *L'Esprit Créateur* 17 (1978), 279–301.

Finally, my thanks to Penguin Books for permitting me to use the Stone translation of *Les Liaisons dangereuses,* first published in 1961, and still in print. I should mention here that, except for the *Liaisons,* all other English versions of Laclos's work and of the secondary sources and primary sources I use are my own.

As always, I would like to acknowledge the support of my wife, Betty. Her patience and understanding, under the pressures of her own career, during the rigors of composing this work made the job easier. And my apologies to my son, Michael, who must have gotten tired of explaining to his neighborhood friends why his Dad was home all the time, instead of at work.

Chronology

1741   Born, Pierre-Ambroise-François Choderlos de Laclos, 18 October, in Amiens (Picardy).

1759   Nominated to the Royal Artillery School at La Fère.

1760   Begins studies at La Fère.

1761   Named *sous-lieutenant.*

1762   Graduates with rank of second lieutenant; asks to be sent to La Rochelle where a colonial brigade is being organized.

1763   Because of peace (Treaty of Versailles), sent to Toul instead.

1765   Named first lieutenant.

1766   Stationed in Strasbourg, remaining there until 1769.

1767   First poem, "A Mlle. de Saint-S***," published in *Almanach des Muses;* named *sous-aide major.*

1769   Sent to Grenoble, where he remained until 1775.

1771   Commissioned a captain.

1772   Nominated to be *aide-major.*

1773   Poems, "Souvenirs," "Epître à Eglé," published in *Almanach des Muses.*

1774   Writes "Epître à Margot" (published in 1776), "Avis aux Princes," which appears in *Almanach des Muses.*

1775   Sent to Besançon, where he would remain, off and on, until 1777.

1776? Joins the Freemasons, in which organization he remains active until the Revolution.

1777   Sent to Valence to establish an artillery school; poems, "Sur cette question...," "Epître à la mort," appear in *Almanach des Muses;* adapts comic opera from Riccoboni's *Ernestine;* promoted to *capitaine en second.*

1778   Returns to Besançon; composes "A une Dame."

1779   Sent to Rochefort and to the Iles d'Aix and de Ré; poem, "Le Bon Choix," appears in *Almanach des Muses;* possibly begins *Les Liaisons dangereuses.*

1780   Named *captaine-commandant;* in Paris on leave, January to June.

1781   Asks for second leave of absence (December 1781–May 1782).

1782   Publication of *Les Liaisons dangereuses* (April); ordered to rejoin his regiment at Brest but returns to La Rochelle on recommendation of Montalembert; corresponds with Riccoboni about *Liaisons.*

1783   Meets Marie-Soulange Duperré (born 15 August 1759); begins *De l'Education des femmes.*

1784   Publishes essay on Burney's *Cecilia* in *Mercure de France;* birth of his son, Etienne Fargeau.

1785   Admitted to the Academy of La Rochelle.

1786   Publishes *Sur l'Éloge de Vauban;* marries Mlle Duperré; moves to Soissons, near Paris; sent to Metz, as punishment for Vauban essay.

1787   In Metz and La Fère; published poems in *Almanach des Muses;* new edition of *Les Liaisons dangereuses,* with poetry and the Riccoboni correspondence.

1788   Still at La Fère at head of his company; takes leave of absence and enters service of Duc d'Orléans; meets Madame de Genlis; birth of daughter, Catherine-Soulange.

1789   Writes Orléans's *Instructions aux Bailliages;* leaves with Orléans for London.

1790   Writes *Exposé de la conduite du duc d'Orléans;* returns to Paris; joins Jacobins and begins editing their *Journal des Amis de la Constitution.*

1791   Writes articles "Du perfectionnement et de la stabilité de la Constitution" and "La Question de la royauté"; resigns from Jacobins (21 July).

1792   Leaves Orléans's service; returns to army as chief of staff of nonexistent Army of Pyrenees; named to, but never assumes, the Governor-Generalship of French colonies in India; also named by Danton as one of the Revolutionary Government's commissioners; battle of Valmy.

1793   Arrested by Committee on Public Safety in March or April; put in L'Abbaye Prison; released soon after the experiments with hollow artillery shells; rearrested in November as Orleanist; sent to La Force, then to Picpus.

1794   In Picpus prison; writes letters home; released in December.

1795   Named General Secretary of Mortgages; writes "De la guerre et de la paix"; birth of son, Charles; lives peacefully in Paris until 1800, during which period he most likely writes an essay on Lapérouse's explorations.

1799   Named General of Artillery by Bonaparte.

Chronology

1800   Assigned to the Army of Italy; sees action for first time.
1801   Returns to Paris.
1802? Writes "Observations sur *Le Fils naturel* [de Lacretelle]".
1803   Returns to Italy in final campaign; dies in Taranto (5 September).

CHAPTER 1

Artilleryman of Letters

I *Introduction to a Life*

LACLOS'S life was one of lackluster achievement and missed opportunity with two exceptions: his marriage and *Les Liaisons dangereuses.* For the biographer, there is little available information and still some confusion about his career, especially during the Revolutionary period (between 1789 and 1800); there is almost nothing on his writings other than the *Liaisons,* and very little on his intentions. Who was Choderlos de Laclos? This question has sustained the renaissance in Laclos criticism since 1905, the date of the two best biographies of that author, those of Fernand Caussy and Emile Dard.[1] Was he Valmont or Danceny (the two principal male characters in the *Liaisons*)? Was he an opportunist or simply an ambitious military officer? Was he an Orleanist or a Jacobin or a Bonapartist or all three? Was he a good writer or just a lucky one? These questions and others compose what has come to be known in Laclos studies as the "enigma of Laclos." There is little doubt, at least on this critic's part, that Laclos was unsuccessful in much of what he undertook. Despite the efforts of his most sympathetic defenders, the portrait one is left with at the end of a study of his life is not flattering. Quite simply, had he not written *Les Liaisons dangereuses,* Laclos would have been relegated to the fourth rank of writers of the last half of the eighteenth century.

He came from an undistinguished, newly ennobled family, made a mediocre career in the least prestigious of the military services, married a woman from a family of no greater wealth or prestige than his own, attached himself to perpetrators of lost causes (notably Montalembert, his military superior, and Philippe, Duc d'Orléans), came within an inch of being guillotined, was named aide-de-camp of a nonexistent Army of the Pyrenees, happened to miss the most important French military victory of his career

17

(Valmy), was named Governor-General of French India (but with no funds, troops or fleet), and, though raised to the rank of general by Bonaparte, died a lonely death of dysentery at the end of the Italian peninsula. The efforts of his biographers to create from this litany of failures a career of unusual variety, energy, imagination, and success are admirable in their virtuosity, but ultimately groundless. The story of Laclos's life — gleaned from the terse records of military archives and from a series of letters written between 1794 and 1803 — is dull, replete with efforts to escape the unalleviated boredom of provincial garrisons, except for the five-year period (1788–93) in which he tried to be, in Dard's phrase, "a precursor of Talleyrand." And yet, from this search to escape boredom came one of the few good novels to be written during the *ancien régime*, a novel of such power that it has succeeded in creating a life for its author that he could not create for himself.

This preliminary chapter will attempt to give a biographical and historical context in which *Les Liaisons dangereuses* may be placed. The remainder of the chapter will reconstruct Laclos's life, evaluate those works he wrote before and after *Les Liaisons dangereuses,* and give a basis from which a study of the novel can be built.

II *In Quest of a Destiny*

Pierre-Ambroise Choderlos de Laclos was born in Amiens (in the province of Picardy), north of Paris, on 18 October 1741. He was the younger of two sons born to Jean-Ambroise Choderlos de Laclos, a secretary to the king, and the grandson and great-grandson of two other middle-echelon bureaucrats who had most likely purchased their title of nobility sometime in the seventeenth century. Not until late in his life did the name Laclos become comfortable enough for the author of the *Liaisons* to use alone; until then, he was referred to and referred to himself as Choderlos or Choderlos de Laclos.

Almost nothing is known of his youth in Amiens or elsewhere. All we do know is that sometime in 1759 he was nominated to attend the Royal Artillery School at La Fère, not too far from his birthplace. La Fère would later become, at the recommendation of another French artillery officer, Napoleon Bonaparte, the national Ecole Polytechnique. The French artillery was well-respected in eighteenth-century Europe, and though less glamorous than other services, was a worthy career for the younger member of a poor, but honorable family. Laclos did not study only cannons and their mechanics, but the arts of attack and defense and the construction of fortifications as well. These interests would be dominant, as we shall see, throughout his career.

While Laclos was studying at La Fère, France was at war with England, and when he left school as a second lieutenant, he asked to be sent to La Rochelle, where a brigade was being formed to defend the French colonies in America. As luck would have it, peace broke out, and Laclos was sent to France's eastern frontier, to the town of Toul, near Nancy. This short tour of duty would be the beginning of twenty-five years of provincial postings ranging from La Rochelle in the west to Grenoble in the east of France. He would leave the borders of France only three times in his lifetime, once with the Duc d'Orléans, to conspire in London, and twice with Napoleon's Army of Italy, finally to die in Taranto in the Kingdom of Naples. His advancement in the ranks would be regular but not exceptional (first lieutenant in 1765, *capitaine par commission* in 1771, *capitaine-commandant* in 1780, the latter title being roughly equivalent to a major in our army; he left the army in 1788 at this rank and did not reach the rank of general until 1799, when Napoleon gave him that commission).

From Toul, Laclos went to Strasbourg where he remained until 1769, when he was posted to Grenoble. By all accounts, his stay in Grenoble (1769–75) was one of the happiest periods of his life. As a young artillery officer with a good name, he frequented the salons of Grenoble society and saw and heard enough to mention, years later, this provincial capital as providing the inspiration for *Les Liaisons dangereuses*. There were and remain many readers of Laclos who believed him, and the Grenoble years, even more intriguing because of Stendhal's affiliations there, have become central to any discussion of Laclos's provincial peregrinations. It was in Grenoble that Laclos, in effect, began his literary career, though he had published a poem, "A Mlle de Saint-S***," in the *Almanach des Muses* in 1767. (It is curious to note that the first line of this poem, the earliest example of Laclos's work we possess, reads: "Dois-je croire ce qu'on m'écrit?" ["Must I believe what people are writing me?"] — a line that uncannily presages the *Liaisons*.) The poems from the Grenoble period were all published in the *Almanach des Muses* and appear in Allem's edition of Laclos's complete works:[2] "Les Souvenirs, Epître à Eglé" (1773; Allem, pp. 447-78), "Avis aux princes" (1774; Allem, p. 481), and his somewhat infamous "Epître à Margot" (1774, but unpublished until 1776; Allem, 478–81). We should begin our survey of Laclos's poetic endeavors with a caveat: he wrote around twenty pieces of verse over a period of about twenty years, and they are of mediocre quality at best. Their interest to us comes from any reflection they may cast on his only masterpiece, *Les Liaisons dangereuses.* Their themes are traditional (love, infidelity, death, temporality, and so forth) and their versification and language uninspired. They are proof of Laclos's desire to impress his social contacts, to show his cultural affinity with the educated nobility, and to remove himself, if only apparently, from an image of the unimaginative artilleryman. However, as mentioned, close readings of these pieces do reveal aspects of Laclos's character and personality not available elsewhere. For instance, in "Les Souvenirs," an uninteresting poem on the value of memory, Laclos, or the poet, describes himself thus: "Moi que l'ennui souvent accable, / ... / J'ai dû chercher ... quelque remède à ma langueur" (Allem, p. 477; "I, whom boredom often overwhelms, ... I had to look for some remedy for my languidness"). In this case, memory serves as such a cure, but there is throughout the works of Laclos a sensitivity to boredom and its effects that is even more fascinating by its insidiousness. Provincial life could be boring, or at least thought to be by those who had experienced the excitement of Paris or else had read about it (Laclos had done both), and for a person with Laclos's agile mind such was most likely the situation. Boredom is a theme and a phenomenon that will have to be examined elsewhere, but it played a significant part in Laclos's response to his destiny.

The most interesting piece written during Laclos's stay in Grenoble was his "Epistle to Margot." It occasioned his first *succès de scandale* and is the only one of his poems to have attracted substantial attention. Written in 1774 and circulated widely, it finally appeared in the *Almanach des Muses* after its notoriety had waned. The reason for the furor is that "Margot" was thought by many to be Madame du Barry, Louis XV's newly installed mistress. She had succeeded Madame de Pompadour, who had died in 1764, as *maîtresse en titre* around 1770. Beautiful and charming, she had been a shopkeeper's daughter and thereby subject to the cruel ridicule of the courtiers surrounding Louis XV. Soon her reputation as a beautiful but uneducated consort spread beyond Paris, and it is this subject that Laclos decided to treat in his poem. The name "Margot" was a lower-class name (du Barry's was Jeanne Bécu), and Laclos's poem ironizes it, insisting that names do not count as much as performance ("Que fait le nom? La chose est tout." "Of what use is a name; the thing is what counts."). So what if "Margot" cannot read, is not a witty conversationalist, is not even recently ennobled; she obviously pleases in other ways.

The poem "Epistle to Margot" is unsubtle and repetitious but worthy of mention, for it is one of three pieces that Laclos would write during his lifetime that would bring him to the harsh attention of the authorities (not counting the articles he wrote during the Revolution which were more dependent for their reception on the instability of public and official opinion): the other two would be *Les Liaisons dangereuses* and *Sur l'Éloge de Vauban (On the Eulogy of Vauban)*. Even though the poem in question was unpublished until after Louis XV's death in 1774, it must have caused Laclos some anguish when he learned of du Barry's anger and saw the possibility of his budding career in the artillery being compromised. But, as Caussy has indicated, there seems to have been no official reprimand from Laclos's superiors.[3] The poem's main interest is in its apparent audacity; Laclos's career, as mentioned above, had several such moments, as if the bored artilleryman was trying to draw attention to his merits, to make himself stand out. And yet, and this point will be elaborated in the concluding chapter of this study, he always withdrew just far enough at the threat of severe reproach: he took two years to acknowledge authorship of the "Epître à Margot" and the *Liaisons* would provide enough false trails to keep him at least partially hidden as well.

For the next five years, Laclos moved from Besançon (1775–77), to Valence (1777), where he helped establish an artillery school, back to Besançon (1778), and finally to Rochefort, La Rochelle and the two islands, Ile d'Aix, and Ile de Ré, where he would reach his peak as a fortification strategist (1779–82). It was most likely while in Besançon that he conceived the idea for the biggest literary flop of his career (his espousal of the cause of the Duc d'Orléans was its equal in the political arena): the adaptation of Marie-Jeanne Ricoboni's insipid novel, *Ernestine,* as a comic opera. René Pomeau tells us that Laclos had obtained the services of an excellent musician, Saint-Georges, and had assured himself of a splendid opening night with the presence of the Queen, Marie-Antoinette, and the King's sister and sister-in-law.[4] The result was an unmitigated failure: only one performance, booed from beginning to end, and so bad that not one word of the libretto has survived! A few more poems, some published in the *Almanach des Muses* ("Epître à Mort," "A une Dame," "Le Bon choix," and a verse critique of Voltaire's *Zaïre,* "Sur cette Question," all in Allem, pp. 483–86, 487, 487–91, 494–95), most likely did little to lessen such a public rebuke. In fact, in "Le Bon choix" ("The Good Choice"), Laclos himself ridicules those who would substitute words for action, no matter how accomplished the word master. Almost pathetically he begins: "Des Beaux Esprits, je hais la vanité; / ... / Soit à la Ville, à la Cour, à l'Armée, / Les gens d'esprit n'ont jamais les bons lots; / Les sots ont tout, même la renommée" ("Of witty dilettantes, I despise the vanity; ... Be it in town, at court, or in the army, intelligent people never have it good; Fools have everything, even fame," Allem, p. 487). At the age of thirty-eight, Laclos was feeling his life and career close in upon him.

It was at this moment that he was sent to Rochefort, near La Rochelle, to work on the defenses along the Atlantic coast. France had been at war with England, at least on the seas, since 1775, and in 1778 an official declaration would be made. The French feared that England would attempt to capture the islands in the Channel and use them for incursions into France. Laclos would spend, off and on, the next eight or nine years in this area. It was while working on the forts on the Isles of Aix and of Ré that he would be under the command of the Marquis de Montalembert, an innovator in the art of fortifications and Laclos's protector until the Revolution. No one is sure, but it is supposed that while on these small, barren, unpopulated islands, Laclos conceived and wrote *Les Liaisons dangereuses* which would appear three years after he arrived there. He had two leaves of absence during this period, one in early 1780 and another in early 1782, both of which he spent in Paris.

At the age of forty-one, less than five years after the disastrous failure of his comic opera, Laclos published in Paris one of the most popular works of any genre to appear in France before the Revolution. The reception and subsequent popularity of this novel, brought out in four duodecimo volumes, must have stunned him. In chapter 2 of this study a close look will be given to this extraordinary work. However, two points must be made here if we are to comprehend the rest of Laclos's career.

First, though the book was an instant *succès de scandale,* it was not banned by the authorities, even after embarrassing keys to the characters were clandestinely printed and distributed. Not until the 1820s would the novel be officially judged to be "outrageous."[5] Second, and perhaps most important for Laclos, he escaped being severely reprimanded for the publication of his novel. In fact, as we shall see, it would be his attack on the military theories of Vauban, four years later, that would bring his army career to a close. The *Liaisons* were published in April 1782; by late May, a letter had been written to Laclos, by the Inspector-General of the Artillery, Gribeauval, to the effect that the author should report to his company in Brest, where he might have less spare time to write such works. However, the Marquis de Montalembert intervened on the behalf of Laclos, whom he called "another myself," and the original orders were rescinded. Laclos returned to Montalembert's headquarters in La Rochelle to resume his duties. And that was the extent of the military's official reaction to Laclos's dangerous book.[6] These two pieces of luck, and luck was to remain Laclos's nemesis and benefactor, meant that Laclos could remain in the army, pursue his career under the auspices of Montalembert, enjoy his newly acquired fame (accompanied, however, by scant fortune), and perhaps use the success of the *Liaisons* to propel him where his birth, lack of fortune, and feeble attempts at writing had not previously been able to do.

III *Le Danger des Liaisons*

Coincidentally with the sudden fame brought by the appearance of *Les Liaisons dangereuses* came the end of the American Revolutionary War and of France's war with England. The island forts, built under the supervision of Laclos and the inspiration of Montalembert, were no longer as important as they had been. Laclos was ordered to La Rochelle to oversee the construction of the arsenal there, a rather lowly employment for the man who had helped establish an artillery school in Valence and who had been in charge of fortifying an important section of the Atlantic coast. Was such an assignment a subtle punishment for having published a disreputable novel? Or was it considered an appropriate assignment for the protégé of Montalembert, an officer increasingly in theoretical conflict with the artillery and the engineering establishment of the French military? These are unanswerable questions; all we do know is that Laclos, less than a year after the publication of the *Liaisons,* found himself assigned permanently to another provincial city, per-

forming another boring job, and absent from Paris and from the
reflected attention of his successful novel. However, in other ways,
his four-year stay (1782–86) in La Rochelle was not entirely
unpleasant.

Soon after his arrival there, he met a young, unmarried woman
who would become his wife in 1786: Marie-Soulange Duperré. Like
Laclos, she came from an established, but modest family. She was
twenty-three when Laclos met her, at least five years beyond the
respectable marrying age for a young noblewoman. It was most
likely owing to her family's modest financial status, and the
absence of an adequate dowry that she was still unmarried.[7] She
seems to have been a charming woman and the relatively indepén-
dent hostess of her family's home. She and Laclos became
acquainted, and he soon became a frequent visitor in the Duperré
house, despite or perhaps because of his reputation as author of the
popular *Liaisons*. Laclos was soon the darling of La Rochelle
society, frequenting the salons of that small town, even being
elected a member of the Academy of La Rochelle in 1785. He became social friends with his military superior, the Marquis de
Montalembert, and his wife, to whom he addressed at least two
poems: "Epître à Madame La Marquise de Montalembert"
(Allem, pp. 471–76) and "A une Dame" (Allem, p. 487).

For unclear reasons, Laclos did not marry Marie-Soulange until
almost two years to the day *after* the birth of their son, christened
Etienne Fargeau, in 1784. Pomeau has suggested that Marie-
Soulange's mother refused to have Laclos in the family, but her
daughter's inopportune pregnancy and the birth of a grandson
must surely have weakened any such hesitation. At any rate, Laclos
and Marie-Soulange did marry in May 1786 and left immediately
for Paris. Laclos legalized his son's name, and the offspring of this
provincial tryst went on to bring the family name honor through his
death in battle in 1814. From all indications, Laclos and Mademoiselle Duperré were devoted to each other, and though the marriage brought no money or family connections, it brought stability
and comfort to the forty-four-year-old army officer.

The period spent in La Rochelle after the appearance of *Les Liaisons dangereuses* was one of some literary activity for Laclos. The
reception accorded his novel had whetted his appetite for success
and the next half decade would be his most productive as a man of
letters. It would culminate in 1787 with the publication, under his
direction, of a new edition of the *Liaisons,* including his correspon-

dence with Madame Riccoboni about that novel, and most of the poems he had been writing since the 1760s. But three works written during the La Rochelle years did not appear in that edition: a review of the novel *Cecilia* by the Englishwoman Francesca Burney, an unfinished memoir on the education of women, and, in some ways the most controversial piece ever written by Laclos, his critique of the military engineer and Marshal of France, Vauban. These pieces, none of them of superior quality, show Laclos's attempts to sustain his reputation as a successful man of letters and polemicist and even as a worthy successor to the great *philosophes* of the preceding generation. One of them would bring him noto-riety and a career change, but unexpectedly so.

The evaluation of Fanny Burney's *Cecilia,* an epistolary novel published the same year as the *Liaisons,* appeared in the *Mercure de France* in April and May 1784 (Allem, pp. 499–521;. The most interesting section for readers of Laclos's novel includes the first few pages which deal with what a novel is and how it works. Writ-ten only a couple of years after the *Liaisons,* one cannot help but make a few useful comparisons between what Laclos likes and criti-cizes in Burney and what he did in his own novel. The essay begins with a justification of the novel as a useful genre, thereby joining a debate by then tiresome, of whether or not the novel was beneficial or harmful to the manners and moral well-being of its readers, especially young ones, more especially young, female ones. Novels, Laclos opines, teach us about private mores, and there is no place else that such information is so effectively available. The novelist, contrary to opinion, is subject to well-defined standards of decorum and verisimilitude, and if these standards are adhered to, then the novel becomes an efficacious pedagogical tool. Though the theater can lay similar claims, only in the novel can the neces-sary luxury of *described* action (as opposed to *represented* and thereby truncated action) be effected. The best novelists have a cer-tain "manner of seeing and thinking" that women especially pos-sess; the inference is that women are often the most successful novelists.

As Laclos begins his résumé of this novel's action, he makes one more observation that furnishes an insight into the special structure of the *Liaisons.* The primary difference between French and English readers, he maintains, is that for the former, character is a function of situation, whereas the English reader seems preoccu-pied with the characters themselves and is only secondarily inter-

ested in the novel's events; or, put another way, the English reader
sees a novel's events primarily as indicators of character, contexts
through which a character is defined, and not as significant in
themselves. In France, on the other hand, "sentiment precedes
reflection," (Allem, p. 504), thereby causing the reader to read
Samuel Richardson for "adventure" and not for characterization.
Such an observation, though fallaciously simplistic, does illuminate
one of the problematic aspects of *Les Liaisons dangereuses,*
namely, the ironic interplay between character and event (in this
case, for the most part, the letters that form the novel), where from
one letter to the next, the reader must refocus his attention and his
critical energies according to each correspondent's view of events.
Laclos obviously felt, as a consequence, that Burney had not succeeded as well as he had: the many minor personages in *Cecilia,*
though adding verisimilitude, "encumber the action and slow the
movement of the novel" (Allem, p. 505).

This essay adumbrates a few other aspects of the novelist's art,
but fails to develop any sort of poetics of fiction. The essay reveals
a literary man, imbued with a love for narrative fiction, steeped in
its traditions and examples: he has read Madame de Lafayette,
Marivaux, Fielding, Richardson, Rousseau, and the very recent
Galatée, a pastoral novel, by his contemporary, Florian. It also
shows that Laclos might have been thinking of writing another
novel, on the power and tribulations of virtue (not exactly a new
topic in 1784), to follow on the success of the *Liaisons.* The essay
on *Cecilia* leaves much unsaid about the writing of fiction, but it
does give a sketchy indication of how Laclos saw novel-writing.

About a year before the essay on *Cecilia* appeared in the *Mercure
de France,* Laclos began another essay that he would never finish,
but to which he returned off and on for ten years. The Academy of
Châlons-sur-Marne had announced a topic for an essay competi-
tion in early 1783 and Laclos saw another opportunity to draw
some attention to himself.[8] The question was: "What would be the
best means to improve the education of women?" The manuscript
of the first two parts of this unfinished essay (unpublished during
Laclos's lifetime) bears the date 1 March 1783 and the epigraph,
from Seneca: "Evil has no remedy when vice becomes custom."
Part I of the essay (Allem, pp. 401–5) is a brief, unfinished preface
to the general question. Laclos begins, not unlike Rousseau had
done thirty years earlier in his first *Discourse,* with a negation of
the Academy's proposition: "There is no way to improve the

education of women" because "our laws and our customs are equally opposed to providing them with a better one" (p. 403). Going further, and again assuming a Rousseauistic vocabulary that would become more pronounced in Part II, Laclos decries the status of the present system of education which in fact deprives women of their freedom, making them slaves to men. In a long sentence, Laclos gives his thesis:

> The question is then to discover whether the education given to women develops or at least tends to develop their faculties, so that their use be to the benefit of society; whether our laws, and ourselves in particular, are not opposed to this development; finally, whether in the present state of society a woman formed by what is called a good education would not be very unhappy in staying in her place and very dangerous if she insisted on leaving it.... (p. 404)

Laclos concludes his prefatory remarks with the comment that, "wherever there is slavery, there can be no education." His logic is that, since women are enslaved by men with the aid of society's norms and laws, it is not in the interest of this system to educate them. Though not designed to please the establishment represented by a learned academy, Laclos's remarks were not as outrageous as they might appear. Neither their tone nor their ideas were new to those who had read Rousseau and his contemporaries. These remarks are much more interesting for the light they shed on the characters of Merteuil and Tourvel in *Les Liaisons dangereuses* than on the history of female emancipation in the eighteenth century. Perhaps it was the recognition of its banality that led Laclos not to submit his essay to the Châlons Academy.

Part II of Laclos's writings on women is the longest of the three (Allem, pp. 406–48). It is in this section that he develops, again à la Rousseau, his portrait of "natural woman": strong, independent, happy, self-sufficient. His aim is to rehabilitate "women disfigured by our institutions" (p. 406; the first-person plural pronouns used throughout this essay seem to refer specifically to *men* and not generally to "French" or "modern" readers). In order to do so, he uses a methodological fiction, the re-creation of an imaginary history of woman, from the pure state of nature to civilized times. The themes Laclos insists on resonate from *Les Liaisons dangereuses,* and include the social roles of memory and imagination, and the denaturalization of female integrity by society's institutions. Chapters 1–8 trace the gradual socialization of "natural" woman. For instance, in chapter 5, "On Puberty," Laclos carefully intertwines the imaginary tableau of a "natural" woman reaching that biological age, and the depiction of a similar development in a civilized society. The girl in the latter society has her physiological and biological development hastened, speeded up by a too intimate contact with the artificial forces of that society. "She seems to surrender to a strange force, and the signs of puberty appear before the individual is developed" (Allem, p. 413). The "natural girl," on the other hand, does not know, from reading unchaste novels, how to blush, or even what a blush means; her imagination is under her control, and she awaits only "the call of nature" and not of society to fulfill her physical and emotional capabilities.

"Natural woman" has the advantages of liberty, strength, and good health. She does not know nor does she care about such empty concepts as "love" or "beauty," concepts devised by a male-dominated society to keep women in thrall. In an observation on the most prized of social myths, Laclos writes: "Love consoles society. [However,] social man acquired this possession [by giving up] all the other advantages of natural man" (Allem, p. 417). In other words, society, by its nature, is insufficient, and needs some sort of supplement, and that supplement is the concept of love. Civilized woman, lured by atavistic memories of her past qualities, and terrified by the future, finds herself trapped in the present, never satisfied, the victim of standards of beauty and respect set up to keep her dependent on the opinion of others and not free to be herself. Victimized by an "unruly imagination" (*imagination déréglée*) that had been sensitized to society's values even before she was old enough to understand or address them, civilized woman is essentially unhappy, defined by others, imprisoned within society's escape-proof prison of values.

At this point in his argument, Laclos interrupts his description of "natural" and "civilized" women to comment on the fiction that he has used as a method to make his argument. He has an imaginary debate with Voltaire and Buffon about whether or not a pure state of nature ever existed, concluding that it did, or, more precisely, that it does. Laclos seems to think that the *idea* of a state of nature exists, and has existed, perhaps as a myth or metaphor, to analyze the idea of the perfectability of the human species. In other words, it is a necessary fiction invented by man to explain what society is *not*. "Is not the instinct of nature, in everyone, something that has been stifled under the weight of our institutions?" (Allem,

p. 431). Fact, idea, instinct: the distinctions become blurred in this chapter, but Laclos clings to this fiction of difference, and the polemical tone of the last three chapters takes on even more force because of it. Chapter 10, on the "Prime Effects of Society," begins with an observation that Laclos had been preparing: "Nature creates only free beings; society makes only tyrants and slaves; each society supposes a contract, every contract an obligation. Every obligation is a fetter which repudiates natural liberty" (Allem, p. 433). This chapter, more than any other, states baldly and emotionally the predicament of women in a civilized world. It is an unstable passage and makes no excuses for its radical arguments. Its message is simple: woman has lost her liberty and has been subjugated to the whims of a masculine-dominated social structure. She is "unnatural," and has thereby been forced to adopt "unnatural" strategies in order to survive, namely, coquetry, adornment, a vivid imagination, and a vocabulary and mechanics of love. Beauty, love, jealousy: all have been induced by society's inherent injustice. In one passage, Laclos gives an interpretation of the "perpetual state of war that exists between women and men" that is, in fact, a reading of most serious prose fiction in France since Marivaux:

Oppression and scorn were then, and would generally remain the lot of women in newly formed societies. This situation remained in force until the experience gained from centuries [of oppression] taught them how to substitute adroitness for force. They felt, then, that since they were weaker, their only weapon was seduction; they recognized that if they were dependent because of male force, men could become dependent because of female sensuality. Unhappier than men, they had to think and reflect more than they; they were the first to learn that sensual pleasure always remains less strong than the idea formed of it, and that imagination went further than nature [or the reality]. (Allem, p. 435)

And so women learned how to make their lot easier, but not to free themselves. The chains remained, though covered with garlands.

The last two chapters develop this re-creation of how men and women came to treat each other. Laclos examines the psychology of dress, the manipulation of desire, and the role of illusion in the sexual relationships of male and female. Part II of his writings on the education of women ends abruptly, but, more than the other two sections, has a methodological and thematic unity which makes his arguments compelling.

Part III of the education essays (Allem, pp. 449–58) was probably written in the 1790s; it gives a program of readings designed to help a young girl prepare for her life in society. "Reading is actually a second education which supplements the insufficiency of the first" (Allem, p. 449). Returning to some of the themes he had first enunciated in his commentary on Burney's *Cecilia,* Laclos suggests that moralists (like La Bruyère and La Rochefoucauld), historians, and novelists should be read. Such works are "dangerous," if read carelessly, but the risk is worth taking, for the ideal results will be a better-prepared, better-protected woman. Like Tourvel and Merteuil, Laclos's young lady should especially read *Clarissa.* Using again the image of supplementing for deficiencies, Laclos observes that "it is for novels to supplement the insufficiency of historiography..., but the choice [of novels] should be rigorous in all aspects" (Allem, p. 454). Let it suffice here to observe that this last — it too unpublished — comment on the societal situation of women does not attain the subtlety or the passion of Part II, but it does give a few indications of the importance Laclos gave to the interplay between fiction and society, and remains an oblique justification of his own novel.

There are available a few incisive articles on the representation of female destiny in *Les Liaisons dangereuses,*[9] but this remains one of the lesser studied aspects of Laclos. There is no doubt, however, that a careful reading of these essays does provide new strategies for the rereading of the *Liaisons.* The only three women in the novel who have sexual relations with men during the story — Merteuil, Cécile, and Tourvel — all represent different facets of the state of socialized women depicted in Laclos's essays. As stated earlier, Laclos's recognition of the inferior social and legal status of women was not an original insight; Marivaux, for instance, as early as the 1720s, had written perceptively on the genius of coquetry and of the necessity of this mode of action in a society geared to the needs and wishes of one sex rather than the other.[10]

These remarks on the education of women remain an energetic revelation of how Laclos saw the mechanisms of his society, and, as Paul Hoffman has suggested, they retrospectively draw attention to an interpretation of the *Liaisons.* In effect, writes Hoffman, Laclos wrote an answer to the Châlons Academy's question *before* the question was ever proposed: "The novel, *Les Liaisons dangereuses,* is a meditation on the condition of woman and calls into question once again the notion of her dignity" (p. 47). In a tightly argued essay, Hoffman in effect relegates the *Essays on the Education of Women* to the status of a companion text to the *Liaisons*. He avoids the easy thesis that the situation of women is a general metaphor for oppression and denial of liberty, adhering firmly to the view that education, if worth anything, should "restore woman to a state of complete autonomy" (p. 48). According to this ingenious interpretation, Merteuil's totalitarian rejection of the values of a sexist society and Tourvel's acceptance, but eventual transcendence of those same values are two possible egresses from the moral and sociological dilemma Laclos uncovers and describes in his *Essays*. Neither is in fact judged successful or unsuccessful by Laclos; however, both are seen as logical alternatives to a no-win situation. The self-delusion nurtured by a dehumanizing social structure provides few other choices to those women who would address the inequities of that structure.

Such a reading of Laclos's thoughts on the education of women gives more luster to them than perhaps they deserve. Nevertheless, they are thematically contiguous to the *Liaisons,* and though never published, would seem to fit into Laclos's possible plan to maintain his heady reputation with a justificatory plea for the morality of his novel. At any rate, since they were not published, there was no way they could effect the kind of attention that the *Liaisons* had brought to Laclos. It would fall to an apparently bland essay on military fortifications to do what even the *Liaisons* did not do: curtail and ultimately end Laclos's military career.

In 1784, The Academy of Dijon chose as a topic for one of its competitions, the eulogy of one of Burgundy's favorite sons, Sébastien Le Prestre, Seigneur de Vauban (1633–1707), Marshal of the French Army during the latter part of the reign of Louis XIV. Known as a great military leader, the initiator of dozens of sieges, and engineer of several hundred forts, Vauban was a symbol to many of the glory — no matter how faded — that had been France's during the last decades of the Sun King's reign. One of the winners of this essay contest was a young Burgundian named Lazare Carnot. He defended Vauban's memory and justified his reputation. In 1786, the Paris Academy announced that its own prize for eloquence would also go to the best eulogist of Vauban (a prize, by the way, that went unawarded until 1790). It was in reaction to this announcement that Laclos wrote and published his letter-essay, "Lettre à Messieurs de l'Académie Française sur l'Eloge de Vauban" (Allem, pp. 543–65). It is not surprising, in

some ways, that Laclos decided to go public in this manner. His
superior and protector, the Marquis de Montalembert, was known
throughout the Royal Corps of Artillery and Engineering as a fer-
vent innovator in the art of construction and reinforcement of for-
tresses. As early as 1761, he had announced the completion of a
lengthy study on *La Fortification perpendiculaire ou Essai sur plu-
sieurs nouvelles manières de fortifier . . . (Perpendicular Fortification, or Essay on Several New Ways to Fortify. . .);* because of its
heretical nature, it would not be published until 1776, and parts of
it not until 1796. Montalembert did publish, though anonymously,
a critique of Carnot's eulogy, but obviously Laclos felt this was not
enough and published his own attack in 1786.

The argument centers on whether or not *fortification perpendiculaire* is superior to *fortification bastionnée.* In other words, is it
better to build forts with large open areas, surrounded with thick-
walled bastions, or smaller forts, even of wood (like the successful
one on the Ile d'Aix), with casemates (enclosures with slits for firing muskets and cannon) which provide protection for those firing
from all sides? Montalembert felt that a smaller force could withstand a larger one as long as the defenders were well-protected by
casemates. (In fact, Montalembert's theories would become standard practice in the midnineteenth century.) It might come as a surprise to learn that such a mundane argument could excite anyone,
but Laclos's unmitigated attack on Vauban did just that. The theses
of his argument are (1) that Vauban should not be counted among
the great men of France, (2) that the present generation should not
accept blindly his outmoded theories and, subsequently, (3) that
the Académie Française should not choose him as a subject for any
prize essays. Laclos strongly condemns Vauban as a general, as an
engineer, and ultimately as a patriot, accusing him of being the
cause for the enormous debt that France was still trying to liqui-
date. He had spent millions rebuilding forts that he had himself
destroyed in sieges; often these same forts were retaken, and
Vauban was then forced, in effect, to battle against his own strategies as he laid siege to regain the lost fortress. Laclos accused
Vauban of having done nothing but continue a tradition begun in
the fifteenth century. Totally lacking in originality, insensitive to
the enormous costs of his endeavors, and equally ineffective as a
defender or attacker, Vauban was a man whose reputation was a
total fiction. More virulently, though, Laclos attacks all of those —
and most noticeably his superiors, other than Montalembert —

who refuse innovation on principle. "Truth," he claims, "comes from the shock of opinions" (Allem, p. 556). The present climate in the Royal Artillery and Engineering Corps represses originality, and rewards mediocrity. The result, he implied, would be continued defeats for the French army, and continued debt incurred by the French government.

There is no effort at reconciliation or temperance in Laclos's polemic; and, there was none in the public response to his letter. Nothing Laclos would do during his life, including his espousal of the Duc d'Orléans's cause, would occasion such a concertedly negative response.[11] The storm hit the same week he married Marie-Soulange. He was immediately ordered to the frontier post at Metz, where his company was stationed. (Laclos had been on official leave from his regiment for about ten years.) No amount of string-pulling, nor entreaties from the perpetrator of this calumny or from his wife succeeded in alleviating his "sentence." The Secretary of War, Maréchal de Ségur, ordered Laclos to remain in Metz; he was not to escape reprimand this time as he had so cannily done after the publication of the *Liaisons.* The official reasons for this official chastisement were two: first, Laclos had published a military treatise without the permission of the Secretary of War (though Laclos had obtained permission from a minor military functionary before proceeding with publication), and, second, Laclos had made unfounded and libelous charges, based on inaccurate data, about one of the great generals of France. So, off he was sent, away from his new bride, to Metz, and later to La Fère, condemned for the rest of his career to the rank of captain and to provincial postings. For the next two and a half years, until late 1788, Laclos would remain the model artillery captain, taking his leaves in Paris, serving with distinction, even being named a Knight of St. Louis in 1787 with a pension of eight hundred *livres,* after twenty-eight years in the service.

The question nags: why, knowing the hidebound traditionalism of his service, knowing the lack of success of a rich nobleman like Montalembert, why write such an egregiously inflammatory essay at that time in his career? Was he naive enough to discount its effect? Did he want to impress Montalembert and his new wife, as well as justify his election to the Academy of La Rochelle? Was he looking for *any* form of recognition that would maintain him in the public eye? All these questions are tantalizing, but unresolvable. No one knows; Laclos left no correspondence from this period.

However, we can venture a deduction. Laclos now had family responsibilities that demanded attention; also, he had a close relationship with Montalembert, the man who had protected him during the flare-up over the publication of the *Liaisons* and with whom his future in the army lay. This latter connection possibly occasioned his polemic against Vauban; no less important was his sense of frustration, at the age of forty-five, as he realized that his liaison with Montalembert might in fact be injurious to his career. Now that France was at peace, Montalembert's idiosyncratic theories would no longer be tolerated. The fort on the Ile d'Aix had served its brief purpose and would now probably be ignored. Laclos's outburst, a rarity for this circumspect maneuverer, was a miscalculation, a gamble that failed. As a result, no longer would he have any chance — short of a major war or a new regime — for advancement or distinction in the service. At this point, after a few years of quiet soldiering in Metz and La Fère, Laclos made a decision to link up with another protector, less admirable, but much more influential than Montalembert.

Laclos spent increasing amounts of time in Paris during his last years in the army and was introduced into, and attended some of the most prominent salons of the capital and of Versailles. It was in these gatherings, aristocratic and high bourgeois, that he came into direct contact with the bitterness and political frustration of these classes. Louis XVI's government was scorned, the king himself despised, but not as much as his queen. There were repeated demands for change, for more power to be given to those classes from which it had been taken by Louis XIV. Sometime in late 1787 or 1788, Laclos met one of the most influential and certainly the most rich of these intriguers, Louis-Philippe-Joseph, Duc d'Orléans (1747–93), cousin to Louis XVI, and, after Louis's two brothers (who would later become, after Napoleon's abdication, Louis XVIII and Charles X), pretender to the throne. Most historians agree that the Duc d'Orléans was a schemer who wanted to put himself on the throne of France, or at least to become Regent. In 1787, his cousin had exiled him from Paris after he had publicly defended the right of the *parlement* to demand explanations for new taxes from the king. His huge palace at the Palais-Royal had become a meeting place for the dissidents, those who were pretenders themselves to the mantle of the great *philosophes*. The heart of what Robert Darnton has called "the Grub Street style of revolution" and the "low-life of literature in pre-Revolutionary

France" was to be found in the cafés that dotted the gardens of the Palais-Royal. Though there is disagreement over the importance of the Orleanist faction's role in the preparation and fulfillment of the Revolution,[12] the Duc d'Orléans, because of his wealth and proximity to the throne, could not help but be a highly visible figure. He would, under his newly adopted name of Philippe-Egalité, vote in 1792 to execute his cousin, only to follow him to the scaffold the same year.

This is the man to whom Laclos tied his fortunes, joining his household as *Secrétaire des commandements,* with a pension of six thousand *livres* (providing a comfortable living when combined with his other, smaller incomes) and an apartment in the Palais-Royal. This post made Laclos the chief accountant and bill collector for the prince; few other members of his entourage would know as much about the fluidity of Orléans's funds than Laclos. It is probably this proximity to the prince's money that gave Laclos the cloak-and-dagger reputation of an *agent provocateur* on which Dard bases the central thesis of his biography.[13] At any rate, he would become an intimate of Philippe-Egalité, actively involved in his politics for about three years. He would accompany Orléans to London in 1790, and supposedly write several of the prince's best-known political statements, finally leaving his entourage in 1792.

The provenance of several of the political writings attributed to Laclos during this period is still questioned. We do know that on his return to Paris from London in 1790, Laclos joined the political club of the Jacobins. He soon became editor-in-chief of their newspaper-journal, the *Journal des Amis de la Constitution.* Before his affiliation with this well-organized and active political party, Laclos most likely had written two important political pieces.[14] One was a purposefully public document of instructions, purportedly written by Orléans in 1789, addressed to those running for the Estates-General, or National Assembly, under his banner (Allem, pp. 660–64). This text was, as Allem states, "a revolutionary document which, issuing from a royal prince, was meant to produce a great effect" (p. 896). The document calls for individual liberties, including freedom of movement and of domicile, freedom against arbitrary arrest and against unduly long detention if arrested, and freedom of the press and of the mails; it also called for a return to the National Assembly of the power to fix taxes, attention to be paid to the national debt, a reform of criminal and civil law, legalization of divorce ("as the only means to avoid scandal from infelicitous marriages or separations"), and so forth.

Laclos also probably wrote, in 1790, a public justification of the Duc d'Orléans (again ostensibly written by Orléans himself, and in the first-person) and his political activities: *Exposé of the Conduct of M. le duc d'Orléans in the French Revolution.* Between 1789 and 1795, Laclos wrote most of the works attributed to him by his biographers, first as a sort of *éminence grise* to the Duc d'Orléans and then, until 1791, as editor of the *Journal des Amis.* None of the pieces are exceptional; some are filled with revolutionary polemics, but they all take a party line, either that of the Orleanist faction or that of the Jacobins, most often covering both parties. Laclos, in such works as *Du Perfectionnement et de la stabilité de la Constitution (On the Improvement and Maintenance of the Constitution,* Allem, pp. 579–92) and *La Question de la Royauté (The Question of the Royalty,* Allem, pp. 596–636), written in 1791 before he left the Jacobins, is revealed as a moderate-to-liberal monarchist (but not, of course, a legitimatist) who had read Rousseau, had class aspirations of his own, and could not believe his good fortune at, for once in his life, being in the right place at the right time. In his political profession of faith, published in the *Journal des Amis* (Allem, pp. 626–31), Laclos lists his reasons for wanting a monarchy, not the least of which is a scarcely disguised fear of demagoguery. After the attempted escape of Louis XVI from Versailles to another country, Laclos saw a perfect occasion for the reinstallation on the throne of the Orléans line, and, of course, for his own installation as privy counselor to the new king or regent. But, once again, Laclos had miscalculated.

The Revolution was heating up; France was at war with Austria, then England; the Jacobins had a schism, and factionalism in general became epidemic. Laclos left the Jacobins, and, as Orléans was increasingly criticized, loosened his ties with the prince (though he continued to live in his apartment at the Palais-Royal). For a while, Laclos apparently was going to try another career in the army. He served in the Ministry of War and was assigned to evaluate (spy on) General Luckner, who commanded the beleaguered Republican armies north of Paris. Laclos became disgusted by Luckner's lack of initiative, incompetence, and bad French (he was German), and reported the sad situation to Paris. While he was on a brief trip to Paris, the Battle of Valmy took place; the French defeated the Prussians. Not unlike Stendhal's hero Fabrice, in *The Charterhouse of Parma,* Laclos "missed" the most famous battle of his career. Valmy was an important victory for the ragtag French army, and in the postvictory flush, even Laclos was hailed as one of the architects of that victory.

During 1792, besides his "participation" in the Valmy victory, Laclos was named chief of staff of a nonexistent Army of the Pyrenees, then named Governor-General of French India, another sinecure with no fleet or troops. Named, through the auspices of Danton, to be one of the Commissioners of the Revolutionary Government of Paris, Laclos seemed to be, once again, lucky. But all was illusion. Fearful of jealous reprisal, he resigned from his position in the army and as Governor-General in 1793, but to no avail. Arrested, along with his former employer, the Duc d'Orléans, on orders from Robespierre's Committee on Public Safety in spring 1793, he spent about six weeks in the Abbaye Prison, until, through petitions and private connections, he was released. For most of the rest of 1793, Laclos experimented, under the auspices of the Department of the Navy, with his invention: the *boulet creux,* or hollow shell, designed for maximum damage to the wooden ships of enemy navies. An impressive invention, this shell would remain in use, with technical variations, of course, until the twentieth century. Despite this success, Laclos's former affiliation with the Orleanists proved too suspect to be ignored, and he was arrested again in November 1793 and would remain in various prisons until December 1794.

It is because of this period of imprisonment that we possess a rare portrait of the private Laclos. Dating from his incarceration in the Picpus prison until his death in Italy ten years later, a rather lengthy correspondence exists, collected and published for the first time in 1904.[15] Writing to his wife during his months in prison, Laclos describes, minutely and repetitiously, the boredom of prison life. He worries about her financial situation (in fact, the Abbaye and Picpus letters are filled with pecuniary concerns) and relates how he is studying and teaching arithmetic and accounting to fellow inmates. These letters are very emotional, filled with a connubial devotion that seems almost to embarrass the biographers of the creator of Valmont. He begs his wife to write him, for he has nothing else to do but wait: "Today, my dear, it is only in order to write to you that I write you (*uniquement pour t'écrire que je t'écris*), for I have absolutely nothing to tell you" (April 1794; Chauvigny, p. 40), and later, "it's only to lessen your worry that I write you this letter, completely empty of anything" (May 1794;

Chauvigny, p. 53). These prison letters also show the normal fears of a man all too familiar with the vagaries and passions of revolutionary politics. Knowing full well that his mail is being intercepted and read, Laclos manages frequent comments on his loyalty to the aspirations of the Revolution.

In July 1794, Robespierre was deposed and executed, and Laclos expected to be released soon; however, for reasons still unclear, he was not. In fact, in late 1794 he was transferred from the minimum-security prison at Picpus to the more severe Petit-Luxembourg. Nevertheless, he was eventually released from custody, without ever having had a trial, in December 1794. The reasons for Laclos's arrest are easily deduced, the essential one being his association with the discredited Orleanists. What is less clear is how he avoided execution himself. At several points in his corresondence home, he seems to feel such punishment is imminent. It has even been suggested that he was blackmailing present government officials with information he had gathered while working for Orleans early in the Revolution. The paranoia of the Terror would certainly have abetted such a scheme. But, we do not know the real answer; perhaps, and this is in some ways the most uncharitable of surmises, Laclos was just not important enough to come to the fore during the frenetic months of the Terror's inquisition (late 1793 to mid-1794). Such a guess goes against the biographical interpretations of Dard and, to a lesser extent, of Caussy, but could, I think, be sustained. At any rate, he survived the most turbulent period of the Revolution, while many of his friends and acquaintainces were losing their heads. He left prison with no more clouds over his own, however, and even managed to obtain compensation for salary and time lost during his incarceration.

The last eight years of Laclos's life were relatively quiet ones. Soon after his release, he was named General-Secretary of Mortgages, an important financial post in Paris, and served in it until January 1800, when Napoleon named him general in the French Artillery. Few records of Laclos's career between 1795–1800 exist. We do know that, soon after his release, he wrote, at the request of the Committee on Public Safety, a white paper entitled *De la Guerre et de la paix* (*On War and Peace;* Allem, pp. 637–54), his last political work. It is an interesting justification for war, arguing that the Republic should continue its wars in order to advance the Revolution and to keep the royalist countries off balance by ruining them financially. It called for natural frontiers for France (the

Pyrenees, two oceans, the Alps, the Rhine) and the complete defeat of England, Austria, and Prussia. The patriotic fervor of the Republic's warriors will carry the day against richer and allied enemies, it asserts. The fact that Laclos himself might benefit from continued war had probably not been too far from his rationalizations; indeed, he did ask for reinstatement into the artillery at this time, but his request went unacknowledged.[16] This was Laclos's last attempt at trying to influence governmental policy on such a scale.

Always aware of changes in the political atmosphere, Laclos managed during this period to associate himself with those who knew and supported Bonaparte. Later, he and his wife would both strongly imply that Laclos had helped to organize the coup d'état of 18 Brumaire An VIII (9 November 1799) that brought the young Napoleon to power. There is no proof of his participation, but proof does exist that Laclos made the claim.[17] Soon after the coup, Laclos was named brigadier general, and assigned to the Army of the Rhine. His letters home during this period describe an old man suffering from rheumatism and hemorrhoids, who had even forgotten how to ride horseback. Surrounded by Napoleon's famous cadre of generals half his age, Laclos wrote letters home that were increasingly plaintive and pitifully ironic when we realize that this is what he had been dreaming for during his whole military career. The letters ring with praise of Bonaparte: "He's your hero, he's also mine; he should be forever the love of all Frenchmen and the object of the whole world's admiration" (January 1800; Chauvigny, p. 210); "it will be Bonaparte who will handle my fate and what he will do will be well done" (February 1800; Chauvigny, p. 217). But, just a little later, Laclos wrote his wife that he had concluded that his own career "has been pretty well fixed at a mediocre level and I am resigned to that fact" (Chauvigny, p. 229).

At two points in these letters written from his first Italian campaign, Laclos reminded his wife — and himself — of the one glorious moment in his past, the publication of *Les Liaisons dangereuses*. The Bishop of Pavia, in Italy, had asked Laclos for a copy of his famous novel. He was unable to find a copy in Italian, but learned that it was widely read in French. He sent a copy, was invited to dinner, and wrote his wife that the bishop told everyone that "the work is very moral and very good to give to others to read, especially young women" (April 1800; Chauvigny, p. 248). So much for fame; Laclos returned to Paris via Grenoble, after having been in his first battle in 1801 at Mozenbano. He remained in France with his wife until ordered by Napoleon to assume command of an artillery brigade in the Kingdom of Naples, stationed in the city of Taranto.

These last two years (1801–1803) in France with Marie-Soulange would be happy ones. He did not want to return to war, and especially to travel the very long distance to the end of Italy's peninsula, but he was a general, and he did have a family, much younger than he, that needed support. Before leaving Paris, Laclos had written a long work, known as *Observations sur "Le Fils naturel" (Observations on "The Natural Son").*[18] This *Fils naturel* is not, unfortunately, the play of the same title by Diderot, but an enormous narrative drama ("roman théâtral") by a mediocre writer named Pierre-Louis Lacretelle. What has attracted recent attention to this piece is a casual comment Laclos made to his wife in a letter dated 16 Germinal An IX (April 1800): "For a long time, the idea for a novel has been growing in my head, and I almost got started on it yesterday.... The purpose of the work is to make popular this truth: happiness exists only within the family.... The event will be difficult to organize and the greatest difficulty would be to make it interesting without making it superficially sentimental [*romanesque*]. I would need the style of the first volumes of Rousseau's *Confessions,* and that idea is discouraging" (Chauvigny, pp. 238–39). Pichois, Versini, and others see the *Observations* as Laclos's first rough draft of such a novel; their arguments are not convincing. Most of the text is a recapitulation of Lacretelle's interminable work. However, toward the end of his remarks, Laclos begins to concentrate on one character of the play, Gourville, who seems to attract him. We will see, in chapter 2, how Gourville's character had been developing in Laclos's imagination since *Les Liaisons dangereuses* and his evolution there of the character of Tourvel. Yet, aside from these few pages, the work, as it has come down to us, is rather pedestrian. It does repeat some themes of Laclos's: the special appropriateness of the novel to analyze private manners, the inherent inability of virtue to fight evil, the superiority of the novel over the theater as a means of sustaining verisimilitude. Whether the text is Laclos's or not, the opinions probably are, and for that reason the *Observations* provide a final, useful glimpse of Laclos the writer.[19]

In May 1803, Laclos left his family, for the last time, and began the long voyage to the Kingdom of Naples to assume his post in

Taranto. The letters home describe a slow and uncomfortable journey for the sixty-one-year-old general. Weakened by the voyage, Laclos contracted dysentery soon after his arrival in Taranto, was ill for several weeks, and soon realized that he would not recover. His main concern was for his family's well-being, and he spent his last days writing letters to all those he knew, including Bonaparte himself (who, after all, was responsible for his being in Naples), urging consideration for the pecuniary straits of his family. This letter, written three days before his death, has a pathetic quality to it when one realizes that the liaisons Laclos had established with his three "protectors" during the last quarter century — Montalembert, Orléans, Bonaparte — had brought him as much misery as reward. "The sad state of my wife and three children, whom I leave absolutely destitute, worries me; but the hope I have that you will help them lets me die more peacefully. That consoling notion, which restores me momentarily, gives me the strength to assure you of the sincere devotion and admiration I have had for you and that I will continue to have until my dying breath."[20] At the end of a two-month illness, Laclos would die on 5 September 1803. His letter to the First Consul would obtain for his family only the smallest of pensions.[21]

Laclos died as he had lived: on the verge of substantial success. However, except for the brief glory that came from *Les Liaisons dangereuses* and his successful marriage to Marie-Soulange Duperré, Laclos's life could be classified a failure, at least in terms of his ambitions and his efforts to attain social, financial, and political success. And yet, one runs the risk of condescension in speaking of the author of *Les Liaisons dangereuses* as a failure. Posterity, the Goddess of the Enlightenment, has blessed the novel, a work that has more than transcended the other ambitions of this artilleryman of letters.

CHAPTER 2

Les Liaisons dangereuses

I *The Book*

SOMETIME in the middle of 1781, Choderlos de Laclos requested a leave of absence from his military duties. He had been stationed near Rochefort, supervising the construction and reinforcement of fortifications on the Ile d'Aix since April 1779, under the command of the Marquis de Montalembert. Despite the opinions of Laclos's best biographers, namely, Caussy and Dard, it is still unclear when he conceived, or, for that matter, when he wrote his only masterpiece. What we do know is that the leave he requested and obtained began in September 1781, and that he signed a contract in March 1782 with Durand *neveu* in Paris to have *Les Liaisons dangereuses* published. Dorothy Thelander has meticulously compared the weekdays which date the letters in the *Liaisons* with the calendars of the years 1778, 1779, and 1780 to conclude "unless strong evidence to the contrary is discovered, that Laclos started work on *Les Liaisons dangereuses* some time between 1778 and 1780, probably in 1779."[1] Fernand Caussy states, with more precision but less authority, that the novel was composed between July 1780 and September 1781,[2] and Emile Dard implies that Laclos wrote the book while enjoying his leave, between September 1781 and February 1782.[3] Finally, René Pomeau, in his recent study, surmises that the book was composed during 1779, 1780, and 1781 while Laclos was on the Ile d'Aix.[4] These are all well-educated guesses, but they, and other hints, do suggest one fact: Laclos wrote *Les Liaisons dangereuses* in a relatively short period of time and published the novel soon after its composition. When he wrote it, he was a captain in the artillery, approaching middle age and unmarried. His career in the military was stagnating; he was not a man of means. The success of this novel, published in early April 1782, in four small volumes, was doubtlessly a heady experience for this bored man.

Of more interest than the date of composition is the publishing history of this novel. Thanks to the detective work of several biblio-philes, we can draw some relatively sure conclusions about the novel's extraordinary popularity, at least during the last two decades of the eighteenth century. The most startling fact, deduced by Max Brun, is that between sixteen and twenty editions of the *Liaisons* were printed bearing the date 1782.[5] Brun cautions that some of these editions might have been published after 1782, but probably at least sixteen appeared between April and December of that year, roughly one every twelve days. For an epoch when the in-tended audience for such a work remained rather limited, this was no small sign of success.

The Bibliothèque Nationale in Paris has a manuscript copy of the *Liaisons,* in Laclos's hand, as well as a copy of the contract he signed with Durand *neveu,* his publisher. The contract states that two thousand copies of Laclos's book would be printed, that the publisher would receive for his services the first twelve hundred copies, that three *livres* or pounds per copy would be paid in royal-ties for the remaining eight hundred, of which Laclos would receive sixteen hundred *livres* total, Durand *neveu* the remaining eight hun-dred *livres.* The contract was normal for the period; obviously Laclos would not, and did not become rich from the sales of *Les Liaisons dangereuses.* To make a large amount of money from writ-ing in the eighteenth century, one had to have the perseverance and cunning of a Voltaire, own a printing establishment, or write copiously and continuously. Our author fell into none of these cate-gories. However, he did soon have a best-seller on his hands. About five weeks after his March 16 contract, Laclos signed another, on April 21, with the same terms. Within one month, Durand *neveu* must have sold at least his twelve hundred copies, if not more. This was the last edition that Laclos personally approved with Durand; however, he probably approved one more edition during his life-time. It appeared in 1787 and included some of his poems as well as his correspondence with Madame Riccoboni.

The first Durand *neveu* edition was printed in duodecimo, in four volumes (measuring about sixteen centimeters by ten centi-meters) of the same approximate number of pages. I mention the size and format because it was felt, as we read repeatedly in various anecdotes of the period, that certain novels should be read clandestinely. It is quite easy to hide a small in-12 volume, roughly six and a half by four inches. (This format was not unique to the *Liaisons;* and, it would be interesting to know all the reasons, if indeed they can be isolated, why eighteenth-century novels were so often printed in such small formats.) The original edition's four volumes had 248, 242, 231, and 257 pages respectively. Volume I contained the fictitious "avertissement de l'éditeur" ("publisher's note") and "préface du rédacteur" ("editor's preface") as well as the novel's first fifty letters; volume II contained Letters 51–87, volume III, Letters 88–124, and volume IV, Letters 125–175. Not a small amount of attention has been paid to the fact that in the only extant manuscript of the *Liaisons,* Laclos divided his novel into two parts, rather than four, ending Part I at Letter 70 (which is Valmont's letter to Merteuil, warning of Prévan's plot to ruin her reputation), and beginning Part II with Letter 71 (another letter from Valmont to Merteuil in which he describes the cuckolding of Vressac). Arguments can be and have been made for the architectural justification of this division. The most interesting point to be made here is that the four-part division, so obviously convenient for the publisher, is also quite justifiable structurally. It is still moot whether that means, as one critic has suggested, that "each part forms a whole, where the divisions coincide with the hinges of the action," and that "at the very birth of the work under Laclos's pen, the dramatic progression was regular and successfully arranged."[6] At any rate, this four-part division was rigorously adhered to (with one exception: a 1782 Neuchâtel edition, which divided the novel at Letter 88, the first letter of Part III of the original edition) by subsequent printers of the *Liaisons.*

The title page of the first edition deserves mention, for, in a subtle way, it gives us a rudimentary strategy for the reading of the novel. One of the most important changes made by Laclos in his manuscript, very near the date of the printing of the book, was to give his novel a new title. The original title was to have been *Le Danger des liaisons;* these words are scratched out in the manuscript, and *Les Liaisons dangereuses* is written in its place. It has been suggested that Laclos had been reminded that Madame de Saint-Aubin had published a novel in 1763 entitled *Le Danger des liaisons, ou Mémoires de la baronne de Blémon,* but it is the ambiguity of the second title that as likely as not attracted him. Not only did the first title have an aura of moralism about it, it also limited the flexibility of the readers' strategic responses.

The subtlety and vagueness of the new title will be discussed throughout this study, but two points should be made here. First, Laclos himself makes reference to the distinction between the titles in Letter 32. Madame de Volanges is writing to Tourvel about the risk she is taking in seeing Valmont. Tourvel in Letter 22 had written of Valmont's apparent act of charity toward a peasant family, of his virtue, of the discrepancy between that act and his reputation as a libertine. She concludes her defense with the comment that "M. de Valmont n'est peut-être qu'un exemple de plus du danger des liaisons. Je m'arrête à cette idée qui me plaît" ("Monsieur de Valmont is perhaps only another example of the danger of ill-considered intimacies. I leave you with this idea, which pleases me." [p. 60]). Madame de Volanges's response in Letter 32 plays on this comment: "Quand il ne serait, comme vous le dites, qu'un exemple du danger des liaisons, en serait-il moins lui-même une liaison dangereuse?" ("Though he should only be, as you say he is, an example of the dangers of intimacy, would he be, for that reason, any the less dangerous an intimate himself?" [p. 76]). The English translation is less ambiguous than the French; for Laclos both *liaisons* and *dangeruses* were terms that could and did refer to persons as well as to events.

The title page of the first edition likewise gives a clue to the multivalent meaning of *liaisons*. Below is reproduced the format of a section of the title page of this edition:

LES LIAISONS
DANGEREUSES
ou
LETTRES
Recueillies dans une Société, et publiées
pour l'instruction de quelques autres.
Par M. C . . . . . de L . . .

J'ai vu les moeurs de mon temps, et j'ai publié ces Lettres.
J. J. Rousseau, Préf. de la Nouvelle Héloïse.

The typographic equality of LIAISONS DANGEREUSES and LETTRES underlines one of the themes of the book, namely, the autonomy of the letters themselves, which is yet another reason why this title was more appropriate than the less subtle *Danger des liaisons*. The title page in fact tells us quite a lot about the novel it presents. The subtitle ("Letters Collected in One Section of Society and Published for the Edification of Others") answers the expected questions about why such a scabrous book was published in the first place. It also strongly implies that what the reader is about to confront only occurred in one small section of his or her society. The quote from Rousseau's famous novel ("I saw the manners of my time, and I published these letters"), published in 1761, serves three functions, all of which will be discussed at length below. First, it reminds the reader of that famous book, the most popular and best-known French novel before the *Liaisons*. At the same time, it is an ironic juxtaposition, unclear until reread after the novel has been read. And last, it ostensibly reinforces the didactic function of the novel, though, again, ironically. In fact, this is the first ironic comment made by the author in a novel that is essentially written in the ironic mode.

This then was the book that appeared in the first quarter of 1782 under the title *Les Liaisons dangereuses*. It was a widely read and discussed novel that brought its author almost immediately to the attention of his military superiors, the first critics of record of his novel. By late May, Laclos was ordered to return, not to Ile d'Aix and his friend, the Marquis de Montalembert, but to Brest where his regiment was officially garrisoned. The *Mercure de France* had announced the novel in late March 1782, and by April a long discussion of it had appeared in Grimm's *Correspondance littéraire.*[7] This was a literary newspaper, with a very limited but influential subscription list. The review begins: "For several years, no novel has appeared whose success has been as dazzling as that of the *Liaisons dangereuses...*" (p. 698). Most of the review concentrates on the unflattering portrait of high society, and Laclos is compared to Restif de la Bretonne and Crébillon *fils*. Yet the author of this article (probably Jacques-Henri Meister who edited the *Correspondance littéraire* between 1773 and 1790) cleverly outlines other approaches to reading the novel that subsequent critics would continue to use. For instance, he draws our attention to the problem of attractive vice. He also is the first to see Merteuil rather than Valmont or Tourvel as the central character of the novel. She is "un vrai Lovelace en femme" ("a real female Lovelace"), says Meister, drawing what will become a common comparison between Richardson's *Clarissa* and Laclos's novel. Perhaps the most significant comment made, however, refers to the impact these "quatre volumes de séduction" will have on their readers. "Quelque mauvaise opinion qu'on puisse avoir de la société en général et de celle de Paris en particulier, on y rencontrerait, je pense, peu de liaisons aussi dangereuses, pour une jeune personne, que la lecture des *Liaisons dangereuses* de M. de la Clos" (p. 700; "No matter how bad an opinion one might have of society in general and of Parisian society in particular, few liaisons will be found, I think, as dangerous, for a young person, as the reading of Laclos's *Les Liaisons dangereuses*"). The very act of reading this novel is dangerous: a theme intentionally employed by Laclos (see chapter 4 of this study for an analysis of this aspect of the novel). Overall, this appreciation of *Les Liaisons dangereuses* is astute and quite useful for the uninitiated reader. It encourages us to read the entire novel, very carefully, and assures us of our reward if we persevere.

Other contemporary reactions to these "four volumes of seduction" were not as favorable. Although Laclos and his publisher had been given a *permission tacite* to print the book,[8] these reactions, including those of his military superiors, must have caused occasional unease. Jean-François de la Harpe, in his own *Correspondance littéraire* with the Grand Duke of Russia, wrote, soon after the publication of *Les Liaisons dangereuses,* that he found the novel and its characters vile, stupid, cold, and lacking in verisimilitude. "Crude ruses, gratuitously revolting crimes, absurd horrors, that is the basis of this work; and yet the author is a man of intelligence.... All the motives of M. Laclos's novel are false and unconvincing" (pp. 703-4). And Moufle d'Angerville, writing in the continuation of Bachaumont's *Mémoires secrets pour servir à l'histoire de la république des letters en France depuis 1762,* though essentially favorable to the artistry of the *Liaisons,* refers to the novel as being "très noir, qu'on dit un tissu d'horreurs et d'infamies" (p. 705; "very black, a veritable pack of horrors and infamies").

Perhaps the best-known reaction to the novel is that of Madame Marie-Jeanne Riccoboni (1713–1792), one of the period's most popular novelists. Authoress of such popular fictions as *Lettres de mistress Fannie Butlerd* (1757), *Histoire de M. le marquis de Cressy* (1758), and *Lettres de milady Juliette Catesby* (1759), Madame Riccoboni was definitely an important personage in literary circles. Laclos knew her before the publication of the *Liaisons,* having done what all critics agreed was a lamentable adaptation of Riccoboni's *Ernestine* for the comic opera in 1777. But more important is the fact that these letters compose the sole record we possess of what Laclos thought about his masterpiece. There are eight letters in the correspondence, four apiece from the two correspondents.[9] Madame Riccoboni's criticisms fall into two main areas: the immorality of the book and the negative depiction of French-women through the character of Merteuil. She begins bluntly: the novel is well-written, but she is sorry that Laclos has used his obvious talents "to give foreigners such an unpleasant idea of the customs of his nation and of the taste of his compatriots" (pp. 686–87). The letter is quite short, almost rudely so.

Laclos's answer is more formal and addresses immediately "la morale de l'auteur." Not unlike his own characters, Laclos uses Madame Riccoboni's own words to turn her arguments around. He seems especially sensitive to Riccoboni's criticism of his portrait of women, and he mentions Madame de Rosemonde's Letter 130 as proof that he is quite attuned to the special psychology of the female mind, as well as to the demands that a male-dominated cul-ture places on women. (This is indeed an extraordinary letter which should be reread in terms of Laclos's essays on the education of women.) He deftly accuses Madame Riccoboni of not being able to read between the lines, and affirms that Merteuil's horrible vices are all the more horrible because he, the author, has made them superficially attractive. "In such a way, in a statue by Pigalle [the most famous French sculptor of the period], one does not perceive without some fear, under a rounded, draped cloak, the very pro-nounced skeleton of the dead man" (p. 688). He enclosed with this letter a copy of his novel.

In her response to this letter, Riccoboni returns to the attack on the grounds that Merteuil wounds the sensitivities of all good Frenchwomen. However, she cannot argue with success: "All Paris hurries to read you, all Paris speaks of you. If it is success to pre-occupy the populace of this immense capital, enjoy this pleasure. No one has been able to taste as much success as you." Laclos answers her criticism, despite the compliments, and again seems almost defensive concerning his portrait of women in the Liaisons. He finds it confusing, he tells his critic, to be accused so caustically (and the implication is that she is not the only one to have criticized him on this point) of depicting women in an unfavorable light. Why, he asks, such sensitivity, if indeed no such women have ever existed in French society? Why avoid the truth? How better to warn against such depravation? Madame Riccoboni, in her longest letter, answers impatiently, but uses a slightly different argument: such characters as Merteuil and Valmont lack verisimilitude. "An extremely perverse man is as rare in society as an extremely virtuous one" (p. 693). Why spend so much talent to depict characters whom the readers cannot — dare not — imitate?

In the last two letters that Laclos wrote to Riccoboni about her reading of his novel, he touches on two points that will be developed in other discussions of this novel, and which imply ways that meaning might be attributed to the *Liaisons*. On his depiction of female ethics and psychology, Laclos admits that he has shown an unflattering portrait, but is it any the less true or valid? (He uses the metaphor of the artist who paints pleasant scenes but as well depicts cliffs, rocky ravines, and volcanoes.) Who is more "truthful," the writer who depicts a Julie or the one who depicts a Merteuil, even a Tourvel? Finally, Laclos states that his object was to reveal the extraordinary recuperative powers of any society faced with the egocentrism of an individual. "The tableau is saddening, I admit; but, it is true, and the merit that I recognize in tracing 'feelings that one wishes to imitate' does not prevent, I think, the usefulness of painting those against which one must defend oneself" (p. 697).

This is a rich correspondence, and it shows that Laclos was much more in the moralist tradition of French literature than he has been given credit for having been. This exchange of letters likewise reveals the influence and understated assumptions of the female reading public. It is Merteuil's perceived "maleness" that seems to have frightened Laclos's female readers, especially Riccoboni, and, to his credit, he sees this character as essentially "female," a fact which explains the insistence (or, as Madame Riccoboni says, "the obstinacy") of his arguments. He would never again write extensive commentaries on *Les Liaisons dangereuses,* but these justificatory letters fortunately support the contention that Laclos's novel was the product of a carefully delineated strategy.

II *The Story*

Les Liaisons dangereuses is a novel about, among other things, modes of seduction. Any more extensive definition of the story elicits, as we shall see, a series of complicated explanations. It is a novel that must be read thoroughly, certainly more than once, before it can be apprehended even on the strictly narrative level. Perhaps the single most obvious example of Laclos's virtuosity (and the most convincing reason for the novel's popularity in our century) is his ability to keep the novel's various subplots delineated, moving coherently and thereby convincingly within their fictional temporal framework. It is for this reason that any résumé of the action of *Les Liaisons dangereuses* appears either surprisingly single-faceted on the one hand, or unnecessarily complex on the other. Nevertheless, as this study is at least partially directed toward those unfamiliar with *Les Liaisons dangereuses,* some sort of summary is needed. Those who have read the novel once or twice might wish to read the following summary as well; Laclos's novel has a complex narrative structure, and it is often surprising how much of it one forgets after each reading.

The novel begins with two fictitious prefaces, one by the putative publisher of *Les Liaisons dangereuses* (p. 17), the other by its editor (pp. 19–22).[10] The ironic aspects of these two prefaces will be examined later; let it suffice here to say that Laclos ostensibly answers some of the major moral questions that he quite rightly saw as being raised on the occasion of the book's publication. There follows a novel, in the Penguin edition, that is almost four hundred pages long. There are 175 letters in the collection, written by a total of thirteen correspondents. The novel is divided into four parts, as mentioned above. The most prolific correspondent is Valmont who writes fifty-one letters, nearly a third of the collection. Merteuil writes slightly more than half that amount (27). The other major correspondents are Danceny (19 letters), Tourvel (25), Madame de Volanges (13), and Cécile Volanges (25).

The primary characters in the novel are the Marquise de Merteuil, a young widow and well-respected member of her society; the Vicomte de Valmont, her "friend," sometime lover, and well-known womanizer; the Présidente de Tourvel, the young wife of a magistrate (a Président, or presiding judge); Cécile Volanges, the very young daughter of Madame de Volanges, who has just arranged her daughter's marriage to the Comte de Gercourt; Madame de Volanges, friend and confidant to Merteuil, Tourvel, and Rosemonde; the Chevalier Danceny, young tutor and eventual lover of Cécile; and, Madame de Rosemonde, Valmont's eighty-year-old aunt, Tourvel's close friend, and ultimate trustee of the whole correspondence.

Most of the story occurs in Paris and in a country home near Paris between 1 August 17** and 14 January 17**. The novel opens with a letter from Cécile to her friend, Sophie, about her recent leave-taking from the convent school they both attended and her impending marriage to an unknown gentleman. Madame de Merteuil's first letter to Valmont, Letter 2, lays out the plan that eventually will lead to their disgrace: Gercourt, Cécile's intended, is to be cuckolded by Valmont *before* his projected marriage. Merteuil's desire is for revenge: she wants to get even with Gercourt (now away in Corsica with his regiment) for having left her for another woman. As it happens (and chance is no small factor in this novel), the woman in question left Valmont for Gercourt, so Valmont should have reason, besides loyalty to Merteuil, for duping Gercourt. However, we learn, in Letter 4, that Valmont is in the midst of his own plot, namely, to seduce the redoubtable Présidente de Tourvel, whose husband is away on business in Burgundy. Valmont and Tourvel are guests at Madame de Rosemonde's chateau and he is whiling away the time with "the most ambitious plan I have yet conceived" (IV, 28). So, in the very first pages of the novel, Laclos has introduced two stories of seduction, both difficult to effect, and both of which will keep the reader's attention on the remaining letters of the correspondence.

Throughout the novel, Merteuil taunts Valmont, deriding his professed reasons for wanting to seduce Tourvel, while urging him to help with her own plot. Nonetheless, for reasons we will see in Chapter 5, Valmont does agree to aid Merteuil while he awaits Tourvel's capitulation. By the time we reach Letter 25, these plots have progressed well: Danceny and Cécile have met and their relationship deepens (Letter 18); Valmont has professed his passion for Tourvel (Letter 23) despite an explicit warning to her from Madame de Volanges about Valmont's well-deserved reputation as a womanizer (Letter 9). Part I of the novel ends with the famous Letter 48 that Valmont writes using the courtesan Emilie as his writing desk. He has left Tourvel's side, but with her promise that she will write to him, and confidently tells Merteuil that he is ready to give her some aid in her own intrigues.

Part II begins as Merteuil sets her finely mechanized plot into motion: Valmont will befriend Danceny, she, Cécile, and together they will spark an affair. But Madame de Volanges learns of her daughter's connection with Danceny and orders it stopped. She pleads with Merteuil for advice. Merteuil tells both mother and daughter that she is their friend, and writes to Valmont of "one of my finest triumphs," that is, the complete and simultaneous control she assumes over the lives and desires of the two Volanges

women, as well as those of Danceny and Gercourt (Letter 63).
Also, in this same letter, two of the plots intertwine, because
Volanges takes her daughter to Madame de Rosemonde's country
home to escape the temptations of Paris, and, at Merteuil's urging,
Valmont returns there to join them. Two important episodes, or
intercalated stories, occur during this sequence, and will be commented on later; they are the so-called "Prévan episode" (Letters
70, 74, 76, 79, 81, and 85) and the "Vressac episode" (Letters 71,
74), stories of other amorous conquests told to each other by Valmont and Merteuil. Part II ends with Valmont's attempt to obtain
the keys to Cécile's room (ostensibly to serve as postman between
her and Danceny), with Merteuil's famous autobiographical letter
to Valmont (Letter 81), warning him of her uniqueness, and with
Merteuil's account of her greatest success at seduction and humiliation, the rejection of Prévan.

All of the relationships formed in the first two parts of the novel
reach critical stages in Part III. Valmont seduces Cécile in her bed-
room (Letter 96) but makes sure that she keeps it a secret while they
both try to arrange a meeting between her and Danceny. Tourvel
flees the country for Paris, an obvious admission that she can withstand Valmont's pleas no longer (Letters 99–101), and finally,
writes to Rosemonde of her passion for Valmont (Letter 102). Merteuil decides to seduce Danceny (Letter 113), and Valmont, piqued,
withholds information from his former mistress. He announces
that Cécile is pregnant (Letter 115), but ignorant of the fact(!).
Through a bold appeal to Tourvel's confessor, Valmont obtains
permission to see his prey at her Paris home.

Part IV begins with Letter 125 in which Valmont recounts to
Merteuil what had been long ago predicted: the capitulation of
Tourvel. This letter also reveals a Valmont confused about his feelings. Tourvel writes Madame de Rosemonde of Valmont's victory:
"Since I shall have lived only for him, to him I shall entrust my
memory" (p. 308). Madame de Rosemonde responds in one of the
collection's most important letters on the assumed difference
between male and female love (Letter 130). At this point, the Merteuil and Valmont correspondence becomes more virulent (Letters
131, 133, 134, 138, 140, 141), and, in one of Merteuil's brilliant
moments, she manipulates Valmont into sending Tourvel a tasteless
letter ending their relationship (the *lettre de rupture;* Letters 141
and 142); this is a mock letter she concocted which was supposedly
written by a lover who explained his weaknesses by repeatedly say-

ing "it's not my fault." Almost simultaneously, Cécile has a miscarriage and Tourvel retires to a convent. In order to buttress her claim of strategic superiority over Valmont, Merteuil sets up a rendezvous with Danceny, at which Valmont, in the only face-to-face meeting the two cohorts have in the novel, surprises her with her young suitor (Letter 151). Insulted, he gives her an ultimatum: to apologize by agreeing to a renewal of their own affair. But she refuses (Letter 152). While the tension of this relationship mounts, Tourvel is becoming increasingly ill at the convent. Her nervous breakdown is recounted by Madame de Volanges, who has learned of her affair with Valmont, to Madame de Rosemonde. Valmont tries to reach Tourvel, but to no avail. At this point, the Valmont-Merteuil relationship disintegrates with the latter's famous scribbled challenge, "Eh bien; la guerre!" ("Very well; war!", p. 358), appended to Valmont's own letter to her (Letter 153).

The remaining twenty-odd letters of the collection recount the denouement beginning with how Merteuil betrays Valmont to Danceny (Letter 162), and how the latter challenges Valmont to a duel and kills him. Before dying, Valmont forgives Danceny and passes his letters from Merteuil and Tourvel to the young man. Meanwhile, back at the convent, Tourvel dies, leaving instructions to have her letters sent to Madame de Rosemonde. Rumors begin spreading about Merteuil, transmitted in part by Madame de Volanges, who remains ignorant of her daughter's own affair with Valmont and thus of the reasons for her desire to become a nun. Danceny, in an attempt to show good faith to Madame de Rosemonde, sends her the letters her nephew had given him as well as his to Cécile (Letter 169). Later he sends Cécile's to him, and Madame de Rosemonde finally has all the pieces to the puzzle. She verifies the rumors that Madame de Volanges has heard about Merteuil's deeds (Letter 172), but still refuses to tell her about Cécile, who enters a convent and becomes a postulant. Danceny chooses a life of celibacy as well and joins the Knights of Malta (Letter 174). In Letters 173 and 175, Volanges recounts Merteuil's disgrace at the Opera where all her former friends publicly humiliate her, where Prévan regains his own social standing, and finishes the correspondence with the information that shortly thereafter Merteuil, having contracted smallpox, becomes terribly disfigured, losing an eye, and fails to win a pending court case, thereby losing her fortune. She flees Paris for Holland with a few jewels.

Before we take a closer look at some of the personages of *Les*

Liaisons dangereuses, a few words should be said about the novel's narrative structure. As the résumé above shows, Laclos had several "plots" going simultaneously. He had to make sure that they were sufficiently complex to be believable, adequately paced to keep his readers' attention, and distinct enough to minimize confusion. All three of these tasks had to be effected without the use of an omniscient, third-person narrator to intervene from time to time in order to keep the reader on the track. (There are about fifty "editor's" notes rather evenly spaced throughout the novel, but they serve primarily to give verisimilitude to the collection, and only occasionally guidance to the reader. More on these notes will be found in chapter 4 of this study.) There are four primary "stories" that occur in *Les Liaisons dangereuses:* (1) the seduction of Cécile Volanges and the cuckolding of Gercourt; (2) the seduction of the Présidente de Tourvel; (3) the attempted reconciliation of Merteuil and Valmont and eventual disintegration of that relationship; (4) the reconstruction, ordering, and publication of the preceding three "stories," that is, the making of the novel *Les Liaisons dangereuses* itself. The brilliance of this novel — and its well-deserved success — is due in large measure to the fact that these four narrative entities can be appreciated separately while at the same time their overlapping makes each individual "story" even more complex and significant.

There are many ways through which Laclos carries off his infinite "jeu de miroirs."[11] Probably the most effective is the extraordinary manner in which he juxtaposes letters, often having the same events recounted by different correspondents. In fact, it is through this strategy of juxtaposition that Laclos's novel shocks most effectively. The process succeeds on two levels, that of description and that of characterization. By description I refer to those letters that belie a carefully constructed and often fallacious self-image that one correspondent creates for the benefit of another. Often, as Seylaz has pointed out, these letters occur in groups: "The groups of letters, their arrangement, their overlapping thus become a remarkable means of creation."[12] The strategy is confidently introduced in the first two letters: Letter 1 being Cécile Volange's incredibly naive note to her friend Sophie, followed by Merteuil's first letter to Valmont in which she outlines her plan to ruin Cécile and her impending marriage to Gercourt.

One of the most successful uses of the juxtaposition strategy on the level of description occurs in the episode of Valmont's putative act of generosity. In his plan to convince Tourvel of his unique character and of his sensitivity, Valmont devises a scheme whereby he will be seen giving money to a poor family that lives on his aunt's estate. He knows that one of Tourvel's servants is following him, so he plans accordingly. Writing Merteuil of his generous act, he concludes: "I appeared not unlike the hero in the last act of a drama. And you will not forget that my [Tourvel's] faithful spy was among the crowd. My aim achieved, I extricated myself and returned to the house. All things considered, I am pleased with my stratagem" (XXI, 58). Immediately following this letter is one from Tourvel to Madame de Volanges recounting the same episode: "My servant was witness to this virtuous act [she fails to write that she had ordered the servant to follow Valmont, a subtle insight into her own character]; he has told me, moreover, that the peasants . . . said that a servant [of Valmont's] had been sent yesterday to inquire into the circumstances of other villagers who might be in need of assistance. If this is so, there is no question here of a mere fugitive pity, aroused by circumstance, but of the solicitude of true charity, of a calculated plan for doing good, a rare virtue in a fine soul" (XXII, 59–60). This obvious and potentially dangerous misreading of events will become one of the hallmarks of *Les Liaisons dangereuses*. Similar juxtapositions occur with such frequency that the reader soon finds himself propelled to read each subsequent letter if for no other reason than to discover if he too has misread the preceding one.

The most consistent use of the strategy in terms of character occurs in the correspondence between Valmont and Tourvel, read in conjunction with the former's letters to Merteuil. There are no letters exchanged between Merteuil and Tourvel, nor do they appear to know each other, though Merteuil seems to know of Tourvel's reputation as an extraordinarily virtuous woman. Valmont understands Tourvel's hesitancies and the moral and social underpinnings of her virtue much better than she. He uses this knowledge to seduce her, and we, as readers, read and watch how Tourvel deceives herself throughout her long struggle. There are two juxtapositions that reveal Tourvel's blindness and helplessness quite well. One occurs at the beginning of the novel (Letters 47, 48, 50) and the other at the end (Letters 126 and 128). The former is one of the most famous scenes in the novel: Valmont writes a "virtuous" letter of love to Tourvel while sleeping with Emilie, his favorite whore, and using her naked body as his desk. The letter is filled with understatement, puns, and other types of word play (see

chapter 4 for a reading of this letter). Tourvel's answer to this letter
ends Part I of the novel, and has to be reread in order to overcome
the remembered duplicity of Valmont's epistle. Such a juxtaposition enhances her vulnerability and thus the reader's anxiety (and
erotic excitement) over her fate.

The second juxtaposition concerns a correspondence between
Tourvel and Madame de Rosemonde. Letter 125 had recapitulated
Tourvel's seduction by Valmont; Letter 126 is Madame de Rosemonde's tardy advice to her friend: "If I can believe what I am
told, my nephew . . . is neither safe with women nor guiltless where
they are concerned, and will ruin them as soon as seduce them. I am
sure you have converted him" (p. 305). As we read this letter,
which had crossed Tourvel's in the mail, we know that it is too late
to save Tourvel from succumbing to Valmont's entreaties, and we
turn quickly a few pages to see how she will respond to her elderly
friend. Such a strategy of juxtaposition is one of the most effective
as well as the most difficult in an epistolary novel with more than
one correspondent. As we shall see in chapter 4 of the present
study, such strategies impose a certain reading of the novel, but
also, if subtle, impress upon the reader the need to formulate his
own readings as well. The "stories" of the *Liaisons* would not end
differently if the letters were rearranged somewhat; however, if
reordered, their narrative power and their credibility would depend
less on the readers' connivance and more on the art of the "editor."
Such would have interfered with Laclos's overall plan, for this
"story," that of the novel's own composition, he saw as being as
important as the rest.

III   *The Correspondents*

To repeat, there are seven major correspondents in *Les Liaisons
dangereuses:* Merteuil, Valmont, Tourvel, Cécile, Danceny,
Volanges, and Rosemonde. There has been a surprising amount of
detective work done, almost from the day the novel was published,
to provide some sort of key as to the "real" identities of these fictional characters. In fact, keys were apparently published almost
immediately upon the novel's appearance. Critics have argued
about whether Valmont was a self-portrait or not.[13] The myth of a
real key establishing a clear relationship between the characters of
Les Liaisons dangereuses and actual, historical personages probably began in earnest with Tilly's publication of a reconstructed

conversation he had with Laclos, in England, in 1789 or 1790. According to Tilly, Laclos told him that he wanted to write a book which "would still resound in the world after I pass on...." He explained that

> ...it was in Grenoble that I saw the original of which my [Merteuil] is but a weak copy, a Marquise de L.T.D.P.M., of whom the whole city spoke as having traits worthy of the days of the most insatiable Roman empresses. I took notes and promised myself to work from them in the proper place and at the proper time. The story of Prévan had happened a long time ago to M. de Rochech..., senior officer in the Musketeers: he was dishonored; people would laugh now. I had in my possession a few little tales of my youth which were spicy enough; I melted together these disparate parts; I invented the rest, especially the character of Mme de Tourvel, which is exceptional. (Allem, pp. 708–9)

This apocryphal anecdote is of interest if only because Laclos's sources for his novel have attracted so much attention. In fact, it is an irrelevant matter whether or not Laclos "copied" his characters from "real life" (some critics have even suggested that the *Liaisons* was a *real* correspondence that Laclos happened to have come across). What is important is how these haunting personages come to have identities within the novel and how the reader participates in their characterization.

From the beginning of this work, Laclos establishes one premise that is essential to the understanding of his characters. His subtitle, it will be remembered, is "Lettres recueillies dans une Société et publiées pour l'instruction de quelques autres" ("Letters Collected in One Section of Society and Published for the Edification of Others"). The English version of the subtitle is correct, for the word "société" in French meant a group of people united by common interests, pleasures, or relationships. Critics from Baudelaire, who called the *Liaisons* a "livre de sociabilité terrible," to Seylaz have insisted on the closed, unstable, and ultimately unhealthy aspect of this small group of people. All the members of this smaller society belong to other such groups which make up the larger social unit that we call Parisian aristocratic and *haute bourgeoise* society of the late eighteenth century. For the purposes of Merteuil's game, the limited society of *Les Liaisons dangereuses* is formed and exists for about four or five months. Like every such social group, this one has its own codes of communication and behavior. Some of these codes, such as those of gossip, of love, and

of seduction are standard to the other societies referred to by
Laclos; other codes, the special set of references used by Valmont
and Merteuil, the particular adaptations established between and
among these particular correspondents, are unique to this smaller
society.

One of the best studies available on this type of literature and of
the special demands it makes on language is that of Peter Brooks in
his *The Novel of Worldliness*. Using La Bruyère's *Les Caractères* as
a source book, and applying Roland Barthes's analysis of La Bruyère, Brooks describes worldliness (or *mondanité* in French) as
"the totality of the forms of man's social existence as they can be
encompassed and formulated by a language and a system which
make no reference ... to sociology, to psychology, etiquette, or
any other specialized, partial, or fragmentary sciences of man as
such. Worldliness, as point of observation and object of study,
is one, a total ethos, the one way of being in the only society
that counts."[14] Brooks concludes his essay on the *Liaisons*
(pp. 172–218) with the suggestion that Laclos's novel was simultaneously an affirmation and a critique of this world view. It is in
leading his readers to evolve their own critique that Laclos hoped to
"edify" other, similar societies.

The seven major characters in this novel have much more in common than they know. It is this commonality that gives their
"société" more than a superficial cohesion, and that allows the
reader to define them and their relationships. Rather than attempt
an analysis of each of these correspondents, a few general characteristics of their relationships, their *liaisons,* should be sufficient to
permit a less naive reading of the novel. Studies abound on the indi-
viduals who create the *liaisons;* few exist on the motives of the relationships that in fact create these characters.[15] In other words, *Les
Liaisons dangereuses* is a novel about connections, not about indi-
viduals. To begin with the obvious, all of the major characters in
this novel (Cécile, Danceny, Merteuil, Valmont, Tourvel, Volanges,
and Rosemonde) exist for and through each other. There is an
absence of solipsism in the *Liaisons* that is even more striking when
we realize that modern autobiography, evolving from its Lockean
origins, was born and developed in the eighteenth century. Even
Merteuil's famous "autobiographical" Letter 81, as we shall see
further on, is directed specifically at Valmont, and is not as self-
indulgent as critics have indicated. There is little of the "affirmation du moi" ("self-affirmation") that one critic has found;[16] it is

the doubtfulness of such an affirmation that made the novel so depressing to Romantic and post-Romantic readers. For the two libertines in the novel, this difficulty of self-affirmation is even more telling, for, despite their observations to the contrary, they, more than any other correspondent, need others, as well as the moral codes of others against which to react. As one critic has eloquently put it, "sans morale, pas de libertinage" ("without morality, no libertinism").[17] Both Valmont and Merteuil are defined in terms of each other and of their prey. Others define them by their appearances, thus they are "unknown" except through mediation, through filters of other people, other values, other relationships. The very trait they think distinguishes them from others, their amorality, has no meaning without the presence of others.

Another characteristic of the novel's main personages concerns a type of blindness, that is, a curious absence of knowledge and often of motive. None of these seven correspondents knows how to use past experience. In fact, all these correspondents are deceived through this blindness, either self- or other-imposed. Cécile's blindness is caused by her mother and her convent education, neither of which prepared her for her tribulations in the novel. Danceny's ignorance is indeed a combination of lack of experience and naiveté. Madame de Rosemonde and Madame de Volanges are victims of their complacency and self-confidence; they have seen the world, believe they understand its dangers, and feel they have nothing to fear from such as Merteuil and even Valmont. Madame de Tourvel's blindness is of more complex origin: secure in her marriage, her carefully structured value system, and in her friendships with Rosemonde and Volanges, Tourvel feels confident enough to allow her sensitive and susceptible self less control than a close association with Valmont should have dictated. Finally, neither Valmont nor Merteuil, as we shall see, are as much in control of their feelings, both their past and present ones, as they believe. All these characters suffer from a false sense of security, which is truly false since they are never secure and, in fact, quite vulnerable. They all dream of lost paradises, and the two youngest of future ones. Merteuil wants to reestablish the putatively perfect love affair she had had with Valmont; Valmont wants the perfect conquest of the perfect woman; Volanges wants the perfect match for her daughter; Tourvel wants to make her marriage succeed, a desire in contradiction to what she has read in *Clarissa* and to what she has heard from Volanges. Finally, Rosemonde wants the happiness of her young friend and the conversion of her favorite nephew. These absolute quests all fail; *Les Liaisons dangereuses* is the chronicle of that failure, and not just of how two evil geniuses ruined the lives of good and virtuous people.

Another lack defines this novel well and that is the absence of responsibility — for the text, for its actions, for its results. From the outset, no one accepts full responsibility for the text's publication (see the fictional prefaces), no one accepts responsibility for the novel's plots (Merteuil alludes to revenge, one of the best excuses for irresponsible action), everyone blames others for his problems (and all of this passing of blame is summed up in Merteuil's "it's not my fault" scheme, Letters 141 and 142). Denying responsibility is in fact denying will and therefore meaningful action; it is fascinating to watch the shadow play of those champions of action, Merteuil and Valmont, as they maneuver each other into accepting responsibility for the disintegration of their intricate schemes. It is only at the end of the collection, when Madame de Rosemonde has all the letters, that one final, responsible act could stabilize a disintegrating world, and she relinquishes this task to an anonymous editor who, in turn, exculpates himself in the first paragraph of his preface (p. 19).

There are other characteristics of the novel's liaisons that are often overlooked in favor of the closer attention paid to the individual characters. At the risk of repetition, it is fundamental that the reader of *Les Liaisons dangereuses* understand that all of the characters in the novel are defined in terms of each other, in terms of *difference*. This makes any judgment of the motives of the characters as well as any final evaluation of their psyches almost impossible. The reader eventually learns that relativity is the epistemological principle that governs his reading of the novel, and that, similar to the failure of Merteuil and Valmont, stabilization of the relationships in the novel, and of his own relationship to the novel, cannot be obtained. Much of the success of this novel is due to this phenomenon. Knowing is supposedly possible, according to the libertines, and according to the propaganda of the Enlightenment, but Laclos, and his fictional editor, argue (or "prove") the opposite. Merteuil especially seems to intuit this frightening possibility. She expends a large amount of time, energy, and force to effect an event (the cuckolding of Gercourt) that is disproportionate to her efforts. The novel depicts the inexorable increase in energy expended, spilling over into other endeavors (namely, the attempt to win Valmont back), as gradually the plotter becomes the victim. This consistent raising of stakes on a worthless game emphasizes and increases the unstable relationships that are the *liaisons dangereuses*. Bored and afraid of boredom,[18] because it vitiates and enervates, the game is joined, but, too late for all concerned, the intractability of the game's rules becomes evident. One of the most important of these rules concerns what one critic has called "the fatality of the secret."[19] If you control secrets, you control knowledge; if you tell secrets, you control others (through the destruction of their carefully constructed appearances). It is the fear of the revealed secret that provides the high level of anxiety in this novel; it is the anticipation of that revelation that keeps the reader (who ultimately will know all the secrets — or will he?) turning the pages. This fascination with secrets, and their corollaries of ruined or preserved reputations, blackmail, and control of the lives of others, unites the seven major characters of the *Liaisons* often against their will or without their knowledge. As Daniel suggests, "it is Mme de Merteuil . . . who really incarnates the magnetism of enigmatic intelligence, the prestige and fatality of the secret. For, the secret, allied with domination, is evil itself."[20] The *Liaisons* is a novel built on the premises of the secret, and yet, always ironic, Laclos published it: the biggest secret was out.[21]

In chapter 5 of this study, we will look closely at the morbid Valmont-Merteuil relationship, but, before ending this discussion on the nature of the relationships in *Les Liaisons dangereuses,* some attention should be directed to the triad that sustains all the other liaisons in the novel. This is, of course the Merteuil-Valmont-Tourvel relationship. More often than not, critics, including this one, divide the book's personages into two categories: Merteuil and Valmont, and the others. This is justifiable, but another perspective helps to underline the interconnectedness of all the novel's relationships, especially the complex Valmont-Tourvel affair. For the purpose of my argument, two "truths" about the triad must be accepted: first, Merteuil's infatuation with Valmont is not reciprocated, and, second, Valmont does love Tourvel. Copious examples supporting these claims can be found in the *Liaisons*. (For example, on the first, see Letters 127, 131, 134, and on the second, reread Letters 100 and 125). Why is Valmont attracted more to Tourvel than to Merteuil? What is it about the young woman that fascinates him? It cannot be her hesitant virtue; he has seen such strategies too often to be interested in them. There are most likely two other possible reasons. Nancy K. Miller has subtly outlined one in her excellent article on Laclos and Rousseau. Expressed a bit differently, it is Tourvel's awareness of her enormous sacrifice that not only attracts Valmont but mesmerizes him. "Like Julie, Mme de Tourvel fears the costliness of passion. In the ideology of the eighteenth-century novel, love (as pleasure) by definition cannot last, but its effects, the suffering (passion), are everlasting.... Love in Mme de Tourvel's system emerges both as alienation ... and immolation, sacrifice being an obligatory function."[22] At one point, Valmont, in a tone of astonishment, writes Merteuil: "But what is the power that draws me to this woman? Are there not a hundred others who would be glad of my attentions? ... Why do we give chase to what eludes us; and ignore what is at hand? Ah, why indeed? ... I don't know, but I am made to feel it is so" (*je l'éprouve fortement*) (C, 236). It is the search for the answers to these questions that keeps him fixated on Tourvel, and his inability to answer them that leads him to his death.[23]

Another reason for Valmont's infatuation with Tourvel is that he is repelled by Merteuil. Merteuil and Valmont do not complement each other; arguably, Tourvel and Valmont do. In other words, the Merteuil-Valmont connection is unstable while the Tourvel-Valmont relationship is homeostatic, at least in terms of their characters as defined by Laclos. Except for their sex (and that is no small difference), Merteuil and Valmont are quite similar: amoral, handsome, intelligent, witty, and fascinated with the social machine. Tourvel, on the other hand, is similar to Merteuil in some ways, dissimilar in others. It is the dissimilarity that attracts Valmont, because her dissimilarity in effect heightens those traits that are similar to Merteuil's, that is, her beauty, her intelligence, her femininity (or womanhood), the intricacy of her arguments, and her commitment to an ethical concept as strong as Merteuil's affected ignorance of one. So, Valmont is an object of strong, equally strong, forces emanating from his *two* female adversaries.

In comments attributed to Laclos on the play of a friend, Lacretelle's *Fils naturel* (1802), Laclos writes about the importance of a well-balanced group of characters: "In a long work, the characters must have that sort of gradation [or distinction] that we notice in ethics as in physical nature; worthless personages would be even more so next to preeminent ones; and the latter would appear gigantic in a group unworthy of them.... This is natural in all well-written novels."[24] Tourvel, then, is a worthy foil to Valmont and Merteuil, even more so when compared to the second group of four correspondents (Cécile, Danceny, Volanges, and Rosemonde). Later, in this critique, speaking of Gourville, one of the "good" characters in Lacretelle's play, Laclos describes him as a man "armed, for the benefit of virtue and the public good, with all the talents of an accomplished schemer" (p. 141). It is this aspect of Gourville, a virtuous diplomat, forced to scheme with a cardinal in order to save his friend and the honor of his superior, that seems to interest Laclos. How better to ensure the success of virtue than to let it be served by the schemer's talents! "Add to the strength of virtue the action of intrigue; to the former's generosity, the gift of letting nothing go unnoticed, of making everything submit and culminate in virtue's plans, in its goal": this is what Lacretelle did in his play with Gourville (pp. 141–42), and this perhaps is what causes Tourvel and Valmont to love each other, against their will. She is guilelessly virtuous; he is a schemer above all else, and together, using each other's charms and values, they are a complementary pair, potentially forming the perfect team that Valmont and Merteuil do not. There are few indications, of course, in the novel that would substantiate such a thesis, except that Tourvel's attractiveness, for Valmont, is inexplicable, *within the novel's own context*. It is the reader's doubt and perplexity that reigns here, and that substantiates the final ambiguity of the book. As Lotringer has remarked, though to a different purpose, "the true enigma of the *Liaisons* does not concern who, in the end, remains master, but rather how has doubt about this question so successfully been maintained."[25] Tourvel, the prude, the bourgeoise, the frank, Tourvel is Valmont's partner; she is the complement that he — and Merteuil — have sought and whose power they refused to acknowledge.

IV   *The Contexts*

Since language is a play of differences, and, by extension, since most literary works play on differences (as well as similarities), the uninitiated reader must be contextually grounded in order to recognize and enjoy this play. Put more simply, the question is: what information is necessary to the first-time reader of *Les Liaisons dangereuses* in order to allow for a reading which is as efficient as possible? For instance, most interpretations of the novel have tended to place it within an historical context that directs its being read as a product of a long socioliterary tradition. This approach underlines the natural antagonism between the two dominant social castes of the *ancien régime,* namely, the aristocracy and the bourgeoisie. The *Liaisons* is thus seen as a text that reflects the tension between a degenerating caste system, and its artistic corollary, Classicism, and a burgeoning, pre-Revolutionary self-conciousness predicated on the myths of success and truth (or virtue).[26]

Such a reading might be called overdetermined. It implies neatly distinct values that the *Liaisons,* in fact, because of the nature of its subject, cannot recognize. This is not to say that the novel lacks an ideology or that knowledge of that ideology is not essential to an efficient reading. André Malraux, in his famous article on Laclos's work, states that "the Marquise and Valmont are the first two [fictional characters] whose acts are determined by an ideology." They know no precedents and presage the characters of Stendhal and Dostoevski.[27] For Malraux, this ideology is that of intelligence; for another of Laclos's more perceptive critics, Henri Duranton, it is libertinism. Duranton's article begins with the question: "Why was *Les Liaisons dangereuses* written?"[28] He accepts none of the traditional answers: certainly not those of the text's two prefaces nor those of other critics based on an extratextual reading of the novel. "The most confident conclusions of traditional criticism seem ... singularly fragile and liable to rejection" when based on readings of this outlandish collection of lying letters (p. 129). Concludes Duranton (and my résumé of his argument deprives it of his admirable subtlety): only in accepting the letters of the *Liaisons* at "face" value, that is, as lies and lies about lies, can we hope to ground ourselves sufficiently to "understand" the novel. There is no underside to the cards, no secret codes breaking through an occasional tear in the veil of lies; the lies are what you see *and* what you get. The only code is a libertine's code, set up in their letters by Merteuil and Valmont and responded to inappropriately by the other characters. There are no depths, only surfaces (pp. 131–32).

This then is the context in which the *Liaisons* should be read, a context created by the novel's protagonists in their letters of record. The pleasure that one gets from reading the novel comes as we watch the transgression of the carefully delineated and articulated principles of the main protagonists by the protagonists themselves. The principles in question form the context, and ground the novel so that satisfactory, but not necessarily definitive, readings of the work may be made. Duranton outlines some of these principles;[29] others have been perceived by Peter Brooks, Georges Daniel, and

André Malraux.[30] If we take a brief look now at letters written by each of the five most important correspondents of the novel — Merteuil, Valmont, Tourvel, Volanges *mère,* and Rosemonde — the context(s) in which their other letters as well as those of the other correspondents should be read will become clearer. The letters I have chosen all appear early in the novel, except for Madame de Rosemonde's; her first letter does not occur until well into the collection. They are those of Merteuil (Letter 2), Valmont (Letter 6), Tourvel (Letter 26), Volanges (Letters 9 and 32), and Rosemonde (Letter 103). My reading of these letters is slightly disingenuous, since they can really be appreciated best after having been *re*read within the context(s) that they are being used to illustrate.

Merteuil's letter is the first she writes, but the second of the collection, tellingly juxtaposed with Cécile's childishly transparent one. As we shall see in chapter 5, this letter calibrates the limits of the Merteuil-Valmont relationship. However, it also introduces some of the principles of the "society" Laclos has chosen to present, thereby providing a context against which the transgressions of those principles — both of the libertines as well as of the nonlibertines — can be measured. In this particular letter, Merteuil outlines the rather simple scheme that will engender the rest of the collection's correspondence. She carefully adumbrates the antagonistic principles of those who live the libertine ethic and those who reject it. The first principle is control, of oneself (don't succumb to "love") and of others, demonstrated by her order to Valmont to return to Paris to aid her in her plans. When a libertine loses the power to control others, she ceases to exist in that mode. Much of *Les Liaisons dangereuses* will be the chronicling of Merteuil's attempts at sustaining that control. Second principle: use secrets. Merteuil confides her plan to Valmont, a plan made possible by her knowledge of restricted information: "Madame de Volanges is marrying her daughter: it is still a secret, but yesterday it was imparted to me" (II, 25). Even Cécile does not know exactly of her mother's plans. Third principle: never forget those who have succeeded where you have failed. Revenge is the motive that initiates Merteuil's scheme: "the hope of vengeance soothes my soul. . . . Let us prove to [Gercourt] that he is only a fool" (II, 25, 26). Fourth principle: use gossip and the threat of gossip. The plan is to cuckold Gercourt, and then to broadcast his shame to everyone. He would become "the laughing stock of Paris" (II, 26). Fifth principle: erotic justification. Any scheme no matter how dastardly may be justified if it satisfies the sexual needs of the perpetrator. Merteuil describes Cécile as an enticement to Valmont: "She is really pretty: only fifteen years of age, a rose-bud. Gauche, of course, to a degree, and quite without style, but you men are not discouraged by that" (II, 26). Merteuil, who finds such description and anticipation an aphrodisiac, knows as well that eroticism is a mainspring to libertine response and action. Sixth principle: plan ahead. The methodological construct of the libertine mode is the project; the intellectualization of desire equals its fulfillment. The project existed before the first letter was written: "I have had an excellent idea and I want to put its execution in your hands.... I am willing to inform you of my plans, but swear first that ... you will undertake no other enterprise till you have accomplished this one" (II, 25). It is the construction and disintegration of this fragile scheme that serves as the narrative scaffolding on which the correspondence is erected. All these principles will be more fully developed as the story progresses, so that the reader can easily provide a context suitable to the production of meaning in this narrative.

Valmont's second letter to Merteuil acknowledges that he knows the rituals of their ethic. In it, he justifies his erotic attraction to Tourvel (while subtly transgressing as well the principle of control). He introduces another of Laclos's themes, that of nostalgia. In this case, it manifests itself in Valmont's description of Tourvel as the "perfect" woman: innocent, honest, loyal, erotic (VI, 32-33). Also, Valmont lays his own plan before Merteuil; it will be a lengthy project, more so than any previous one, but all the more delicious in execution and result. Another principle is strongly supported: Humiliate the victim. Tourvel will not only lose her virtue, says Valmont, but she will have to prostrate herself before her *new* God: "I shall indeed be the god of her choice" (VI, 34). Her capitulation must bring with it complete surrender of all values, liaisons, and desires. "I cannot be really happy unless she gives herself to me" (VI, 34), and that includes any "happiness" with Merteuil.

In one of her early letters, Tourvel reveals how much work Valmont has created for himself. In earlier letters, she had outlined her virtuous values to Madame de Volanges (Letters 8, 11, and 22), and in this, her first written communication with Valmont, she puts these values to the test. Explaining a moment of weakness to Valmont, she shows herself naively confident in her ability to withstand any untoward emotions, since she is confidently protected by virtuous intentions:

Accustomed to inspiring none but honourable feelings, to being addressed only in such terms as I can listen to without blushing, to enjoying, as a result, a security which I have the temerity to believe I deserve, I have never learnt to disguise or to repress the emotions that I feel.... No, Monsieur, I am in no ... danger. (XXVI, 68)

By her very words, within the context of her earlier communications with Volanges *mère,* Tourvel has prepared the way for her own seduction. By this point in the narrative, the information accumulated makes the reading of Letter 26 an exercise in dramatic irony. *We* know, she does not, how her very self-confidence and vaunted values will be used to make her defeat even more sweet to the victor. No knowledge of the ethical values of the upper bourgeoisie in late eighteenth-century France is necessary to understand the enormity of Tourvel's blindness to the threat represented by Valmont.

The mechanisms of such deception devolve from the values enunciated by the novel's two guardians of public virtue: Mesdames Volanges and Rosemonde. These values have the inflexibility of cliché, but imply an ethical universality that makes them easily recognized — and accepted — by contemporary and modern readers of the *Liaisons.* As with most of the letters in the collection, a second reading of Madame de Volanges's two letters to Tourvel resonates with irony. Yet even an initial reading reveals the steadfast blindness of any rigid system of ethical values. Responding to Tourvel's letter in which she had revealed that Valmont was at Madame de Rosemonde's country home with her, Volanges writes: "...I do not think I can avoid saying a few words to you concerning the Vicomte de Valmont.... What, after all, could there be in common between you and him?" (IX, 37). She knows Valmont well — "his conduct is the outcome of his principles" (IX, 38) — but can no better counsel Tourvel on how to protect herself than she had counseled her own daughter. "Persuade his aunt not to keep him any longer," she pleads, or leave the chateau yourself. He is duplicitous and thus dangerous to someone of your openness, she argues (IX, 38). But, most significant in this letter of warning is the attention paid by Volanges to public opinion and rumor. "Scandalous stories [about Valmont] do not reach you in your modest and secluded world; ... society has begun to notice Valmont's absence, and ... it is known that he has spent some time alone with his aunt and you, your reputation lies in his hands — the greatest misfortune that could ever befall a woman" (IX, 38). Volanges fails to realize that though the argument of possible disgrace might have worked for her, it will not — cannot — work for a woman as self-confident and as little aware of certain of society's codes as Tourvel. Like Cécile, Tourvel has developed her own code of behavior; but, whereas Cécile's is the result of ignorance, Tourvel's is evolved from a firmly held, well-reasoned value system, almost asocial in its essence.

In her longer Letter 32, Volanges attempts a more subtle warning directed to Tourvel's unique personality and philosophy. She uses the religious vocabulary of the devotee, adapting her style to Tourvel's, in order to convince her: "God alone can absolve us of our sins the moment we repent; He alone can look into our hearts"; do not try to usurp this function (XXXII, 76). Suddenly, in the middle of this brilliantly contrived — and telling — letter, Volanges shifts registers and returns to her original argument, namely, that Tourvel does not have enough experience of the social world to read correctly Valmont's subterfuges. At this point, she digresses into a description of the social world to which Laclos refers in the epigraph and subtitle he chose for his novel. It deserves to be quoted in its entirety. Why do I, and others, she asks, deal with Valmont if he is so evil?

In so far as I am concerned, I have no more excuse than anybody else. Certainly I receive Monsieur de Valmont as he is received everywhere: there you have another of the thousand inconsistencies that rule society. You know as well as I do that one spends one's life noticing them, complaining about them, and submitting to them. Monsieur de Valmont, with an illustrious name, a large fortune, and many agreeable qualities early realized that to achieve influence in society no more is required than to practise the arts of adulation and ridicule with equal skill. He has more talent for both than anyone. In the one instance he uses it to charm: in the other to intimidate. No one respects him, but everybody flatters him. Such is his position among people who, with more discretion than courage, would rather humour him than cross swords with him. (XXXII, 77)

This passage, when juxtaposed with Madame de Rosemonde's ineffectual advice to Tourvel, reveals the dilemma that virtuous young women, and, in fact, most of "polite" society faced because of inconsistent and complex codes of behavior. Rosemonde, in her first letter to Tourvel, almost takes for granted her young friend's seduction; previously aware of what was going on between her nephew and his prey, she could discover no means to end it. "But what can I do except admire and pity you?" she writes nostalgically. "If the day should come (God forbid!) when you have the misfortune to succumb, believe me, my dear, you must at least leave yourself the consolation of having fought with all your might" (CIII, 243). Coming late in the book, this letter but echoes the helpless "advice" that both Cécile and Tourvel receive from their elders. "I can do nothing," avers Rosemonde, at least admitting what Volanges's startling portrait early in the novel had but intimated. The Valmonts (and Merteuils) of their society fed on their own desires to be recognized, flattered, (favorably) gossiped about, charmed. How can one condemn the naive trust of a creature formed by the very ethical structure one helps to sustain? It takes courage, and no one in this novel — except for the unworldly Tourvel — possesses that courage. Self-examination is too frightening, and therefore ignored. And so, Tourvel does succumb, and Volanges remains ignorant; Rosemonde learns all, but too late for herself, her friends, or her society.

The essential contexts of *Les Liaisons dangereuses* are fully delineated early in the novel. The false questions of "morality" versus "immorality," maliciously misleading and slyly introduced in the two prefaces, take us nowhere in the production of this text's meaning(s). As we will examine more fully in chapter 4 of this study, Laclos deliberately confuses all the readers of the novel, fictional as well as "real." A teleological apprehension of the novel's "lesson" or "moral" is impossible; ethical values are relative and protean. When they become clichés, they lose meaning; and any attempt to give them meaning, just like any attempt to read the *Liaisons* in a "traditional" way, is a failed enterprise before it begins.

CHAPTER 3

Motifs of the Epistolary Novel

I *Introduction*

*L*ES *Liaisons dangereuses* cannot be adequately read or appreciated unless the reader has some knowledge of the narrative subgenre of which it is perhaps the best example. Laclos chose the format for his fiction with care and used its possibilities and limitations in such a way as to question the format's very viability as well as to ascertain its uniqueness. There are few works of fiction that so confidently and persistently draw attention to their own methodology and results than does the *Liaisons*. For this, and other reasons, we should pause to consider the techniques and themes of epistolary fiction before proceeding to any further analysis of the novel.

The letter novel was, with the memoir novel, a dominant fictional narrative structure of the eighteenth century; however, there is a curious paucity of critical material available on its properties and performance. The specific demands that the epistolary format made on a writer, as well as the specific advantages which it affords, have been developed and analyzed in part by Jean Rousset, François Jost, and most recently by Janet Altman.[1] The purpose of this essay, though closely tied to theirs, is somewhat different: it seeks to discover those elements that consistently informed epistolary fiction of the seventeenth and eighteenth centuries in Europe. Its aim is not only to seek a coherent evaluation of the properties of an important narrative subgenre, but to try as well to understand better the relationship between epistolary and other types of narrative fiction. The epistolary novel is especially interesting to study in these terms because unlike the memoir novel, the diary novel, the autobiographical novel, and other similar types, it is a narrative subgenre whose formal distinction is most definite

70

and unambiguous (a letter has certain characteristics and the form elicits common responses from its readers). Also, the format imposes obvious and formidable restrictions on the novelist (for example, first-person narration, a continuous present tense, problems of character development, and so on). The novelist's reactions to those constraints can teach us a good deal about the development of prose fiction in the eighteenth and nineteenth centuries. Finally, the epistolary novel is relatively isolatable historically (flourishing roughly between 1650 and 1800). Obviously, the genre has remained with us, but it can be convincingly argued that its dominance as a narrative form began with the publication of Guilleragues's *Lettres portugaises (Letters from a Portuguese Nun)* in 1669, and waned perceptibly after the appearance of *Les Liaisons dangereuses* in 1782. All of the narrative techniques and thematic variations had been hinted at, if not fully developed, by the time of Laclos's novel. Such a historical fact facilitates the critic's task, especially when speaking of tradition and reader competence. Ideally, this analysis will not only aid in the discussion of *Les Liaisons dangereuses,* perhaps more significantly, it will help us to understand why certain themes and procedures were persistent in the eighteenth-century novel, why some became attenuated, and why many predominated until the midtwentieth century.

The procedure is simple enough: to isolate what will be called *dominant motifs,* a group of denominators which help define the epistolary novel. These denominators are redundant, that is, they occur frequently, but not necessarily in any aprioristic order. They are constraints under which the novelist must construct his work, and to which he has to adapt his subject matter. These motifs are *not* exclusive; there may be others. However, it is certain that the few discussed here are essential to epistolary fiction. Also, they interlock and subsequently overlap somewhat. In other words, they are not hermetic categories; in fact, it is this very quality of overlapping that makes some epistolary works such complex artifacts. Finally, the aim of this introductory essay is to furnish indices of what a reader should look for in reading a fictional epistolary text. The admittedly idiosyncratic isolation of these motifs reveals a fact to which we shall return briefly at the end of this essay, namely, that they are not unique to epistolary fiction; rather, it is their conjunction, their strategic development in letter novels that is of interest. It is to be hoped that a result of such work in this area would not be the separation of epistolary fiction from other fictional modes, but its determination within the context of the whole of fictional narrative.

The motifs are five: *absence*, epistolary fiction being par excellence a literature of absence; *time*, almost every epistolary novelist has to deal with chronology, since awareness of time is a *sine qua non* of the correspondents; *exchange*, a term which encompasses all social aspects of epistolary correspondence; *reflexivity*, the thematic use of first-person narration which is, of course, the dominant narrative voice of epistolary fiction; and, last, *epistolarity*, or the writers' awareness that they are writing and reading, and the effect that such narrative self-consciousness has on the work and its reception.

II   *Absence*

Epistolary communication has no justification unless the letter writer is separated from his receiver. Correspondence exists because of separation; consequently, when the reasons for this separation are removed, the need for correspondence ceases. (Examples of such situations include the end of a voyage, the reunion — and often marriage — of separated lovers, and so on.) Conversely, should absence become permanent, that is, should the chance for reunion or reconciliation become increasingly dim, the correspondence also ceases (for example, the death of one of the correspondents). In Montesquieu's *Lettres persanes (Persian Letters),* published in 1721, a tale of the voyage of two Persians to Europe, Usbek's interminably delayed return to Isfahan (Persia) weakens his authority over the seraglio, and results in the infidelity and subsequent suicide of his favorite wife, Roxane. By the end of the correspondence, Montesquieu has made us aware that nine years have passed since Usbek's departure from Persia, and that his absence is no longer just a pretext for writing, but the very subject of the increasingly weak epistolary contacts he has with the harem: "One thousand leagues from me, you dare judge me guilty; one thousand leagues from me, and you punish me," one of his wives writes him in a letter late in the novel.[2] But this theme had been sounded much earlier in the correspondence; in Letter 22, we read, "As Usbek travels further from his harem, he turns his head toward his cherished wives; he sighs, he cries; his pain increases, his suspicions become stronger" (p. 52). In Letter 96, the chief eunuch writes Usbek: "Come back, my lord, return home with all the signs of

your authority. Come, ... come, ... come, ... come," (p. 199).
Such passages illustrate one of Montesquieu's preoccupations in
the *Lettres persanes:* the misuse of power. Usbek's absence from
his harem, his attempts at sustaining his waning influence through
an active correspondence, and his ultimate failure to do so are all
variations on this subject.

This example as well illustrates several of the permutations of the
motif. There are three categories of absence: (1) geographical or
spatial; (2) temporal or chronological (an aspect which will be discussed more fully when we look at the motif of *time*); (3) psychological (the latter, a feeling which evolves from a *deficiency* created
by spatial or temporal separation, the result of which is often the
weakening of memory and the subsequent weakening of desire).
The letter exists only because of absence; it is a sign of absence, and
an attempt at the attenuation of the time and space which separate
the correspondents. When this attenuation is effected, the letter, as
we have noticed, is no longer necessary. One of the first and most
successful letter novels, Guilleragues's *Lettres portugaises* (1669),
shows how a unique correspondent uses the letter to recreate a presence through memory, and then allows absence to solve her despair.
She mentions "the cruelty of absence" in the first few lines of her
first letter. Continuing, she laments: "What! this absence, to which
my sorrow, as ingenious as it is, cannot give a sufficiently horrible
name, will then deprive me forever from looking at those eyes in
which I used to see so much love, and which made me know those
sensations that overcame me with joy, that replaced everything for
me, and that finally satisfied me?"[3] Her correspondent's dis-
inclination to respond to her letters plus the therapeutic effect of
writing itself combine by the end of the correspondence to cause
Mariane to cease writing, and in the fifth and last letter, she can
confidently say: "I am writing you for the last time" (p. 61).
Absence has served both as a motive and as a destroyer of an epistolary connection. Every correspondence is predicated on the
assumption that contact must be maintained; as that assumption
weakens, the correspondence is no longer justified.

Another popular French novel of the second half of the eighteenth century begins: "I must flee from you, mademoiselle, I
know that: I should have done so earlier; or rather it would have
been better never to have seen you. But what can I do today? How
should I proceed? You promised me friendship; understand my
confusion, and advise me."[4] "Il faut vous fuir": so begins Rous-

seau's *Julie, ou La Nouvelle Héloïse (The New Heloise),* a novel in which Saint-Preux and Julie often reflect on absence. As Saint-Preux says to Julie at one point:

I received your letter with the same passion that your presence would have caused me; and, carried away by joy, a useless piece of paper replaced you [*un vain papier me tenait lieu de toi*]. One of the greatest evils of absence, and the only one against which reason is useless, is the concern one has for the actual state of the loved one.... Oh absence! Oh torment! Oh bizarre and fatal state where one can enjoy only the past, and where the present does not yet exist. (pp. 216–17)

This is one of the most perceptive comments on absence made by a fictional correspondent. Saint-Preux knows that only the letter can attenuate absence, and yet it reminds him cruelly of the absent one. Rousseau and other epistolary novelists of the period were aware of this ambivalence of receipt, and used it constantly for dramatic effect.

   Paul Ricoeur has suggested that "desire is but an imagined pleasure," an intellectualization of sensuality. Desire, sexual and otherwise, is analyzed, deferred, effected, and often destroyed in the epistolary fiction of the seventeenth and eighteenth centuries. The impossibility of satisfying one's needs, because of absence, is one of the most poignant and most consistent motifs of letter novels.

   One final example of the motif of absence should suffice to underline its significance in letter fiction. One of the most popular novels of the eighteenth century was Madame de Graffigny's *Lettres d'une Péruvienne* (*Letters from a Peruvian Woman,* 1747). There are few novels in which the motif is so pervasive. Briefly, the story is about Zilia, a Peruvian vestal virgin, who is kidnapped on her wedding day by Spanish freebooters. She is rescued soon by French sailors, placed on a ship to Europe, and arrives in Paris where she is adopted by a gentleman, Déterville, and his family. Zilia is the novel's only letter writer, and most of the letters of this collection are directed to her absent lover, Aza, Prince of Peru. From the beginning, Zilia uses the letters as the only means by which she can stay in contact with Aza's memory: "I shudder at your absence";[5] "How your presence would embellish such pure pleasures," she laments on seeing the beauties of nature (XII, 107); "Nothing will assuage the weight of your absence" (XVI, 136); she is ever aware of the "immense void of absence" (XVII, 150–51).

Such expressions and observations abound in the novel. All the permutations of absence (temporal, spatial, psychological) are examined by Graffigny, and the novel builds to a verisimilar climax as we anticipate the meeting, in Europe, of the captured Peruvian prince and the lonesome vestal virgin. In her last letter to Aza, as she is awaiting his arrival from Spain, Zilia combines the themes of absence in one last burst of epistolary emotion. The distance between her and Aza is lessening, as he nears Paris. The correspondence which had sustained her, is ending, but she writes to the last moment:

> ...I interrupt my letter almost at each word to run to the window, [but] I do not stop the writing which soothes the emotion in my heart. You are nearer to me, it is true, but is your absence less real than if the seas still separated us? I do not see you, you cannot hear me; why then would I stop conversing with you in the only way that I can? Only a moment more, and I will see you; but this moment does not yet exist. Ah! Can I make better use of what remains of your absence than in painting for you the intensity of my love for you! (XXXIII, 307-8)

And here the correspondence between Aza and Zilia ends; when Aza arrives, his fiancée finds him changed: he is Europeanized and a Christian, and they cannot be married since they are related and Catholic dogma forbids it. Aza leaves again, and now the heroine's heart begins to mend the *longer* he is away. Absence has become a palliative.

This work, and the others, could not exist without the motif of *absence*. Rousset agrees: "With an absence, create a presence, such is the paradoxical power both of passion and of the letter."[6] Desire, one of the major themes of all fiction, is caused by absence in the letter novel. The correspondence creates, sustains, and eventually attenuates desire. And this is one of the paradoxes which also determines this type of fiction. As Altman has shown, "the letter's mediatory property makes it an instrument which both connects and interferes.... As an intermediary step between *indifference* and *intimacy,* the letter can move the correspondents in either direction."[7] And the use of *absence* —its permutations and ramifications — helps to define the success of the epistolary work.

III   *Time*

A dominant motif of epistolary fiction that is in many ways contiguous to the motif of *absence* is that of *time*. There are few other forms of fiction where time plays such a necessary and pervasive role.[8] We have already mentioned how the temporal aspects of absence are as significant as the spatial and psychological ones. The fact that Usbek stays away for nine years is essential to the denouement of the story. And time can attenuate to the point of nothingness a desire which was once all-consuming (for example, Mariane's love in *Lettres portugaises)*. The reader of epistolary fiction is confronted constantly with temporal considerations. The presence or absence of dating and the specificity of dating (for example, "late morning," "the next day," "February 26th, 1723," "mardi," and so on) are aspects of this motif. The ordering or arranging of letters, the difference between the time of occurrence, the time of narration, the time of reading, the time of response, and so forth, are part of the epistolary novelist's art as well. The most complex and durable of letter works are those that not only confront the convention of fictional time, but direct the reader's critical attention to its importance as a thematic element.

Janet Altman has best outlined some of the temporal aspects of epistolary discourse. One of the necessities for what she calls "epistolarity" is "temporal polyvalence": the moments of epistolary fiction include the "actual time that an act described is performed, the moment in which it is written down, the respective times that the letter is dispatched, received, read, and reread" (p. 153). Perhaps the most difficult task for the epistolary novelist is to objectify successfully what goes on between letters in a fictional correspondence without confusing the reader, and without making the fictional construct too obviously artificial. Nevertheless, as Christian Metz has affirmed, ". . . one of the functions of narrative is to create one temporal sequence within another."[9] Consequently, the novelist has to take into account the different "narrative times" of his story. There is first the time of the correspondents, of the *Erzählzeit,* during which they write about what happened or was going to happen to them. There is the *erzählte Zeit,* or the time of the story which they reproduce. There is next the time of the editor of the correspondence in which he organizes the letters, in effect reordering the correspondents' time. Finally, there is *our* time, the real reader's time, which Austin Warren refers to as "reading time or 'experienced time,' "[10] which is still, however, controlled by the novelist. The confusion often occurs because epistolary novels are *about* the process of reading (as we shall see in our discussion of the motif of *epistolarity*), and our chronological experience, or experience of reading time, is often a subtle reflection of those of the fictional readers. Three brief examples should suffice to show how persistent the problem was and how varied the solutions.

There is an impossibility of a dialogue in the present between epistolary correspondents: the letter is not read as it is being written (not by its intended recipient, at least). This time lag makes the present "unseizable"; it is almost impossible for the narration to be simultaneous to the event. However, one early and important epistolary novelist concluded that "writing to the moment" was the only desirable and verisimilar epistolary discourse. In the preface to his third novel, *The History of Sir Charles Grandison* (1753-54), Richardson explains the necessity of such a lengthy correspondence: "The nature of familiar letters, written, as it were, to the *moment,* while the heart is agitated by hopes and fears, on events undecided, must plead an excuse for the bulk of a collection of this kind. Mere facts and characters might be comprised in a much smaller compass: but, would they be equally interesting?"[11] He had stayed with the same chronological method which he had used in *Pamela,* the almost simultaneous recording of emotional experience. He tried to reduce the difference between narrated time and time of narration, between the *erzählte Zeit* and *Erzählzeit,* but, the technique's lack of verisimilitude bothered him. We know this from a letter he wrote to his friend and advisor, Aaron Hill, in 1746, about *Clarissa Harlowe,* which he was then composing: ". . . I have shorten'd much more than I have lengthen'd; altho' it will not appear so by this first Parcel. . . . The fixing of DAtes has been a task to me. I am afraid I make the Writers do too much in Time."[12]

Nonetheless, the apparent spontaneity of letter writing was a characteristic which Richardson felt was essential to a "successful" correspondence, as he attests in his letter manual, *Familiar Letters* (1741). "Writing to the moment" established a bond of intimacy between reader and fictional letter writer and at the same time allowed for the depiction and analysis of "a minutely particular account of thoughts, actions, and accompanying circumstances at such frequent intervals as to make up a current record rather than a retrospective summary."[13] Richardson's purpose was to describe the *present,* and how Pamela's responses to it affected her moral education. The private experience, the immediate response, and the literary formulation of that response were his subjects.

Guilleragues's *Lettres portugaises,* it will be remembered, was a

very short novel, composed of five letters written by Mariane to her
absent lover. She is writing in the present, the inescapable epistolary tense, but she is fascinated by the *past*. Memory is her last,
weak link with her absent lover. "...I committed my life to you as
soon as I laid eyes on you, and I feel no small pleasure in sacrificing
it to you now" (I, 39). The fear that he will never return emphasizes
her hypnotic attachment to the past, yet the remembrance of what
was is of little solace: "My sorrows can receive no consolation, and
the memory of my pleasures overcomes me with despair. What! all
my desires will then be for nothing, and I will never again see you in
my room with all that ardor and passion that you allowed me to
see?" (II, 44). Mariane uses her tenuous epistolary connection with
the departed lieutenant to try to reestablish what was: "I remember," "remember me," "I am content with your memory," "I was
struck by a cruel memory": these are typical of the phrases of
memory which appear throughout the five letters. As Janet Altman
has written, "meaning is not relative to one time but to two or
more" (p. 172), and this is Guilleragues's point: the past has meaning only in terms of the present. Another example occurs in Marivaux's *La Vie de Marianne* (*The Life of Marianne,* 1731–41), which
is also a memoir novel, where the past dominates the writer. Just as
Pamela would concentrate her efforts on an ever-threatening
present, Marivaux's Marianne carefully and nostalgically tries to
reconstruct a nebulous, and almost legendary past. The result is a
unique use of the possibilities of epistolary fiction, where the present is the dominant tense and time, to recreate the past for psychological and social reasons.

Our last example, that of *Les Liaisons dangereuses,* is the most
complex one. This novel can be said to present an effort by its two
main protagonists, Valmont and Merteuil, to apply the principles
of libertinism in the control of time, more specifically, to control
the *future.* In his essay on Laclos, Georges Poulet has outlined
Laclos's use of time.[14] The "real subject" of the *Liaisons,* he
argues, is "to discover whether the course of behavior one follows
always coincides with the course one had planned to follow, and
whether the actual present proves to be the result of the past in
which one had decided upon it, and identical to the idea of it one
had then conceived" (p. 57). The *Liaisons* is the story of a *project,*
"but of a project that turns out badly. The man who projects a
mastery of time is mastered by time" (p. 64). Even Valmont's and
Merteuil's own "creation," the novel of letters itself, escapes their

vaunted control. We are told by the "editor" that "this work, or rather this collection of letters, which the public will perhaps find too voluminous in any case, contains nevertheless only a very small portion of the correspondence from which it was drawn.... I have tried, in fact, to retain only those letters which appeared necessary either to an understanding of events or to the development of the characters" (p. 19). And the "understanding of events" encompasses the problem of time: "arranging in order such letters as I allowed to remain (an order which almost invariably follows that of the dates...)." And yet there must have been some temporal tampering: how was he (the "editor") to know in which order letters that bore the same date were written, received or read, or how soon afterward they were answered? Most importantly, how did he decide in which order *we* should read them? T. Todorov has written several pertinent essays on the temporal aspects of the *Liaisons,* and he has shown that the ordering of the letters, post facto, created a novel within a different temporal sequence than the one that the correspondence might have originally illustrated.[15] Todorov's point is a brilliant one: there are, or were, *two* novels: that of Merteuil and Valmont, and that of the "editor." The former tried to control the future; the latter carefully recorded their failure.

In the second letter of the collection, and her first, Madame de Merteuil speaks to Valmont of the future, introducing it as the key temporal coordinate of the novel: "Come back, my dear Vicomte, come back, ... I am willing to inform you of my plans [*projets*].... The hope [*espoir*] of vengeance soothes my soul. You have been irritated as often as I at the importance Gercourt attaches to the kind of wife he wishes to have, and at the stupid presumption that makes him believe that he will escape his inevitable fate" (II, 25–26). *Espoir:* hope and the anticipation of what is to occur. This is one of the temporal mainsprings of epistolary fiction (we saw it in the *Lettres d'une Péruvienne,* for instance). The letter writer is caught in the present; he cannot even control who is going to receive his letter (an important distinction between the desired recipient and the real recipient should always be kept in mind), much less how events will change the meaning or import of his letter's contents. *Souvenir:* memory and the attempt to recreate the past. This is another key temporal pole which is present in all epistolary fiction (again, we saw it in the *Lettres portugaises,* for example). And, again, the writer, trapped in the present, an "impossible present" as well, has to hold his temporal relationships together, connecting the past with the present with the future. "The *now* of narration is its central reference point, to which the *then* of anticipation and retrospection are relative."[16] Yet, the correspondent emphasizes the temporal mode which interests him the most, as this brief analysis of the works of Richardson, Guilleragues, and Laclos has shown.

In his classic study, *Time and the Novel,* A. A. Mendilow speaks of "the illusion of simultaneity and of the concurrent prosecution of anticipatory and retrospective movements produced within the unitary, consecutive medium of fiction."[17] The novel, epistolary and otherwise, has to come to grips with "the three characteristics of time — transience, sequence and irreversibility" (p. 32). Every good novelist is soon aware of the problems of reproducing time in a fictional context, and success means that his artifact will meet one of the minimum standards of artistic creation. Time isolates man, and the epistolary structure, because of the separation of the letters in a collection, emphasizes this isolation. Each novel, each letter has its own chronological system, based on the length it takes to create it, to read it, to send it, to write it, to receive it. Each exchange has its own time, each whole correspondence its own. Letters are attempts at stopping time, of controlling it, and in the epistolary work, time is shortened, lengthened, intensified through the processes of memory and anticipation. The chronological juxtaposition of letters, the use of *anachronologie,* the interposition of anticipatory and retrospective references, for instance, all give witness, not to the limitations of the present tense and of first-person narration, but to the possibilities which an awareness of the fictional functions of *time* affords.

IV   *Exchange*

Every epistolary correspondence is based on the notion of *exchange,* the third of our dominant motifs. In fact, exchange is one of the elemental structures of any society. The linguist, Emile Benveniste, in several essays,[18] has thoroughly examined the question of linguistic exchange, and has provided us with a useful set of denominators which clarify some of the problems one encounters when studying this motif. "Every man taken as an individual sets himself as *me* in relation to *you* and *him*" ("Language," p. 1). This is one of the linguistic oppositions inherent in discourse. No language is possible without the presence of the person implied by *I*. However, "as soon as the pronoun *I* appears in a statement, it evokes, explicitly or implicitly, the pronoun *you* and the two together evoke and confront *he*. In this moment a human experience is relived..." ("Language," p. 2). Given the fact that the first person is dominant in epistolary fiction (another aspect of which we will explore when we look at the motif of *reflexivity*), Benveniste's remarks are of real pertinence.

In his best-known essay, "Subjectivity in Language," Benveniste proposes an answer to the question: to what does language owe the property of communication inherent in it? He eschews the description of language as an "instrument of communication," because that implies that man and language are distinct, separate; they are not. "We can never get back to man separated from language..." (p. 224). Likewise, "consciousness of self is only possible if it is experienced by contrast.... Neither of the terms [*I/you*] can be conceived of without the other" (p. 225). Each use of the *I* is different, defined by the discourse in which it occurs, and by the interlocutor with whom the *I* exchanges linguistic signs. As he concludes in his essay on the code of signals established by bees and its difference from human language, "society is ... the condition of ... language" ("Animal Communication," p. 54). *I* and *you, je* and *tu* form a polarity which is not only distinctive of, but absolutely essential to, the successful functioning of an epistolary exchange. Each *récit* is a point of contact, and a willing exchange between writer and reader, and letter fiction illustrates this premise to a striking degree.

At the basis of the modern novel is a belief in the integrity of social commerce. Correspondence is a social act, a basic contract which is either sustained (through confidence and trust) or betrayed (through gossip or the misuse of trust). The exchange does not need to be exactly reproduced in order to be artistically effective. *Les Lettres portugaises, La Vie de Marianne,* most of *Pamela,* Crébillon's *Lettres de la marquise de M*** au comte de R***,* to name just a few, are all fictional correspondences where we see but one writer. Sometimes the writer may mention the regular receipt of letters, as in Crébillon's work, or not, as in Guilleragues's, but no matter: the *idea* of exchange, whether absent or not, is what defines these novels and all other letter works. Exchange is a socializing process, a demand placed on the person who would make himself a part of a given society. In fact, some have seen the metaphorizing of exchange in literature as reflecting the basic economic order of Western society, especially capitalism. Roland Barthes, for instance, has referred to narrative as being essentially a type of merchandise: "one tells a story in order to receive something in exchange."[19] This something is a form of recognition; writing a letter is an act of recognition which demands recognition in return.

However, the letter has as well the potential for deception. Besides the letters themselves, writers exchange personae. Roger Duchêne, in perhaps the best work on nonfictional epistolary writing, his study of Madame de Sévigné, the seventeenth-century chronicler of high society, reiterates that the good letter writer is the one who knows how to present himself well to others. The ability to communicate sufficiently with others through letters is proof "of a success whose object is less the art of writing than the art of living in society."[20] Correspondence is always a two-way street: "each letter remains opaque for those to whom it is not addressed" (p. 31). Every letter has to recognize the existence of the Other, and each judgment has to take into account the relativity of values. Every letter is a rhetorical piece, designed to convince the recipient of the validity of the writer's point of view, and every letter is as ambiguous as is the relationship between the sender and the receiver of the letters. Despite the usefulness of Duchêne's observations, we must remember that fictional correspondents exist only through and by their letters; there is no way we can verify the sincerity of their remarks except through a study of what they say and how they say it. The historian and the biographer are of little use to us here.

In Marivaux's novel, when Marianne warns us repeatedly that she does not know how to write, that all she wants to do is to relate privately to her friend how she got to be the *comtesse de* ***, we must be careful, as indeed must her confidant, for there is a good chance that she is falsifying the bond of good faith which an exchange should strengthen. The same observation may be made about the two scoundrels in *Les Liaisons dangereuses,* as they change their styles and thus their personae, adapting them to the intended recipients of their messages. Their success depends of course on the violation of one of the traditional truths of private epistolary correspondence, that of trust. And, in *La Religieuse (The Nun),* Diderot presents a woman, a nun against her will, who wishes to impress a man of influence with her innocence and sincerity in order that he might effect her release. However, we are soon aware that she uses coquetry mixed with forensic rhetoric very successfully to make her case, again falsifying, no matter what the justification, the exchange.[21]

Such possibilities of deception, either gentle or not, create an obvious tension between narrators in most epistolary works (and in those with only one narrator the tension is between the personae of that narrator, or between the real reader and the fictional letter writer). This is one of the hallmarks of letter fiction, and it is one of the reasons that so many epistolary novels can be read with pleasure today. We, the readers of fiction, watch the protagonists adapt themselves and their responses to the exigencies of each individual exchange. There is complexity of motive and execution implied by the writing and exchanging of letters. In a letter to a female friend of his in 1746, Samuel Richardson made the following observations on the positive values of epistolary exchange:

What charming advantages, what high delights, my dear, good, and condescending Miss Westcomb, flow from the familiar correspondences of friendly and undesigning hearts! ... I make no scruple to aver, that a correspondence by letters, written on occasions of necessary absence, and which leaves a higher joy still in hope, which presence takes away, gives the most desirable opportunities of displaying the force of friendship, that can be wished for by a friendly heart. This correspondence is, indeed, the cement of friendship: it is friendship avowed under hand and seal: friendship upon bond, as I may say: more pure, yet more ardent, and less broken in upon, than personal conversation can be even amongst the most pure, because of the deliberation it allows, from the very preparation to, and action of writing.[22]

Conversely, Richardon's witty contemporary, Samuel Johnson, had the following remarks to make on Pope's correspondence: "There is ... no transaction which offers stronger temptations to fallacy and sophistication than epistolary intercourse.... A letter is addressed to a single mind, of which the prejudices and partialities are known: and must therefore please, if not by favoring them, by forbearing to oppose them."[23] Both these observations show the complexity of motive and execution implied by the writing and exchanging of letters. The best epistolary novelists were likewise aware of these possibilities, and their works are source books of the variety of epistolary communication.

V *Reflexivity*

A student of epistolary fiction soon discovers that it is a paradoxical narrative form. Letters can serve as connectors *and* barriers; an epistolary novel is composed of discrete temporal units while giving the impression of a disjointed chronology, and so forth. Another apparent contradiction which appears often concerns the fourth of the five motifs to be treated, *reflexivity.* This term refers to the thematic use of the dominant voice of letter works, the first person. The *I* is always present in the letter novel, and as we saw when we discussed *exchange,* the *I* almost always implies a *you.* However, and this is where the paradox becomes more apparent, the constant use of the first person by necessity introduces corollary themes of self-analysis, autojustification, and self-awareness into the narrative. In an essay on Jacques Lacan, David Funt explains how the French psychoanalyst has used Benveniste's theories of discourse to support his own theories on the psychological "subject":

I can only be defined in terms of locution.... It is in identifying oneself as a unique person pronouncing *I* that each of the locutors poses himself as 'subject.' ... [The *I*] ... is the key to the system of internal references which bind the discourse together. It is also this system of references which serves to define the individual in terms of the particular linguistic construction which he uses in order to announce himself, what we may generally call his style. Through the use of the *I* the individual appropriates the language and appropriates it in a way which distinguishes him, that is, rejects distinction.[24]

The *I,* then, is central to all discourse, and epistolary fiction emphasizes this linguistic truth. However, the epistolary novelist who would remain faithful to his form in its purest sense has to walk a very narrow line in order to keep his work from falling into absolute autobiography (as in Marivaux's *La Vie de Marianne,* Goethe's *The Sorrows of Young Werther,* or Senancour's *Obermann*) where the *I* is absolute, or into a situation where the *I* becomes subdued by the multiplicity of correspondents and events which override the development of this motif (for example, in Smollett's *Humphrey Clinker*). Despite these pitfalls, and there is no doubt they caused problems, one of the advantages of the epistolary format was to allow for flexibility in the use of first-person narration.

If the point of all correspondence is to communicate, then what? Once contact is established, once absence is attenuated and time temporarily and illusively controlled, what concerns the writer most if not the chronicling of his reactions to events, personalities, and emotions? In perhaps the best-known letter of *Les Liaisons dangereuses,* Letter 81, Madame de Merteuil gives Valmont a detailed account of her emotional education. Critics have suggested that such a personal epistle was out of character, that Laclos's insertion of this letter added a note of *invraisemblance* to the carefully delineated portrait of his main protagonist. Such an observation does not take into account one of the main themes of the *Liaisons:* the creation, by Valmont and Merteuil, of personae, through their letters, which would sustain and nurture that primary concern of their society, one's reputation. Merteuil's letter is integral to the novel's construction, and not a casual addendum. More importantly, it underlines the self-consciousness of Laclos's heroine, and implies that every letter has at least some part of auto-justification. "And where, after all, is the achievement of yours that I have not a thousand times surpassed?" (p. 179). This sentence opens her "autobiography," and the remainder of the letter gives us the best — and only — explanation of how Merteuil became the corrupt and destructive woman she was. "I might say that *I have created myself" (Je puis dire que je suis mon ouvrage)* (p. 181, my italics): she has created of herself an artificial, powerful and dangerous superwoman, who is the product of intense reflection and self-analysis. The theme pervades the novel, and this letter, almost exactly in the center of the collection, forces Laclos's readers to recognize as essential to the understanding of the whole book this doomed urged toward self-definition.

At the other historical pole of our inquiry's scope, the same argument can be made about the *Lettres portugaises.* Jean Rousset describes this novel in the following manner: "Made for communication, epistolary language turns toward solipsism and turns back on the letter writer; it leads, despite its destination, to narcissistic introspection, a process that answers one of the needs of first-person narration. The impassioned letter transforms itself thus into a soliloquy on passion, on the individual suffering through his passion."[25] Though he sees this work as a paradoxical example of epistolary fiction, an opinion which my study should belie, Rousset's comments illustrate aptly the importance that this motif has in that novel.

The *I* is dominant in *Lettres portugaises,* and every reference (temporal, spatial, or psychological) uses the *I* as a reference point. "Cease, cease, unfortunate Mariane, vainly consuming yourself..." (I, 40), she admonishes herself in one of her exercises in self-pity, a corollary of excessive reflection. By the middle of what Spitzer has called a series of "monologues intérieurs,"[26] Mariane's attention has turned almost completely from her absent lover to herself. "What will become of me, and what do you want me to do? ... Alas! how much I should be pitied for not being able to share my sorrows with you, and to be miserable all alone" (III, 47). The letters are no longer a means of communicating with an absent lover but a means of talking to and about oneself. The lover's absence is always in her mind, but Mariane is using the therapeutic device of writing to assuage her anxiety. "I am writing more for myself than for you, I am looking only to console myself" (IV, 58); her correspondence had not only sent messages to an absent lover, but had led her out of her own despair.

The motif of *reflexivity* can be traced in such novels as *La Vie de Marianne, La Nouvelle Héloïse, The Sorrows of Young Werther, La Religieuse, Obermann,* and Balzac's *Le Lys dans la vallée (Lily of the Valley).* It is a dominant motif, but one tied closely to the others, uniting with them to form a creative paradox. As Benveniste has taught us, the discourse of *I* requires *you* as a counterpart. This is an inarguable point; however, an analysis of epistolary fiction has revealed that preoccupation with self, coupled with the desire to express that preoccupation, is one of the informing principles of this narrative subgenre, and would continue to influence the development of prose fiction, through such forms as the *journal intime,* the interior monologue, and so forth, for generations, though the fictitious *destinataire* would disappear and be replaced by another, more subtle type of imaginary reader.

VI *Epistolarity*

The last motif to be examined is that of *epistolarity.*[27] This term refers to that aspect of the letter novel which is the writer's awareness that he or she is *writing* or *reading,* and the effect that this narrative self-awareness has on the whole work. A study of this motif reveals that epistolary novelists showed varying amounts of sophistication in its use, but that, increasingly, it became a dominant motif which would tie epistolary fiction to other types of fictional narration. The most obvious examples of this type of narrative self-consciousness concern the physical problems of writing. Where does one get pen, ink, paper, pencil, and other such necessities? Where does one get the time and place to write? How dependent is one on the services of the mails and/or messengers, and so on? One of the most amusing of such problems occurs in Madame de Graffigny's *Lettres d'une Péruvienne,* where the heroine, Zilia, "writes" seventeen of her thirty-eight letters with knotted strings, called "Quipos," before, happily, she learns to write in French.

There are numerous other examples of the awareness, on the part of the fictional correspondent, of the problems of obtaining the time, place, and materials with which to write. Of course, the more sophisticated the novelist, the more careful he or she is to take such matters into account. Richardson's Pamela has some special problems because she is a prisoner of Mr. B., but, as she tells us at one point, "good Mr. Longman gave me above forty sheets of paper, and a dozen pens, and a little phial of ink; which last I wrapped in paper, and put in my pocket; and some wax and wafers."[28] She later has to worry about where to hide her journal, finally making a corset of clandestine correspondence. In *La Nouvelle Héloïse,* Julie and Saint-Preux are always waiting for the mail to arrive, asking for forwarding addresses, mailing letters, writing in secret, out-of-the-way places. In *Les Liaisons dangereuses,* both Valmont and Merteuil, as well as other correspondents, apologize for lengthy letters (Letter 76), provide utensils for others to use (Letter 73), forget portable secretaries (Letter 71), look for paper and ink substitutes when deprived (Cécile in Letter 69), and so on. Even in the spare, intense *Lettres portugaises,* Mariane has to hurry her letter because a messenger waits (IV, 57), and apologizes for writing a long letter at another point (III, 50). The competent novelist knew that a certain verisimilitude was expected by his readers; after all, letter writing was a common and very popular occupation in the seventeenth and eighteenth centuries. The lengths to which he or she went to account for the inconsistencies between the actual composition of letters and a fictional situation determine how sensitive such a writer may have been to the criticism of *invraisemblance.*

On another level, fictional correspondents are often acutely aware of their epistolary styles. A careful study of many letter manuals of the sixteenth, seventeenth, and eighteenth centuries has revealed that one of the stylistic expectations of personal epistles was that of affected negligence (a "style négligé").[29] The readers of these manuals were told to write as they spoke: "Naturalness above all else" (Vaumorière, p. vii). Later, this same manual advises that, though letters should be carefully written, "it is not necessary that our exactness go so far as to make people think we work diligently at writing. All should appear natural in a letter, and it is absolutely essential that any artistry be hidden'' (p. xxv). In another manual written a half-century later, Mauvillon advises his readers that everyone likes to be flattered, but to hide carefully the flattery so that it does not shock and so that the recipient "cannot ... discover your plan to insinuate yourself; for that is essentially what should not appear.... In general, the epistolary style must be lively, natural, simple, and concise. No matter what type of letter one writes, rhetorical commonplaces must be avoided. Conversation does not demand such decoration. And, after all is said, what is a letter, if not a written conversation?'' (pp. 256–58). Marivaux's Marianne is no one's equal in applying such strategies. Writing to her friend, she asks: "Where do you think I would find a style? ... How does one go about obtaining one? Are those I see in books the best? Then why do they displease me more often than not? Does the one I use in my letters seem adequate to you? Then I will write this [letter] in the same way.''[30] Such affected carelessness and doubt about how to write are hallmarks of a good deal of epistolary fiction. These examples from the letter manuals and Marivaux's novel are intended to show the tradition in which the epistolary novelist was working, and how the letter novel was expected to illustrate this "antirhetorical" tendency in favor of sincerity, frankness, and stylistic simplicity.

As mentioned in the discussion of the motif of *exchange,* there is always the possibility of deception in a correspondence, and the apparent disorder and inattention to stylistic devices are often but another mask. The most notorious case of stylistic deception is the various styles used by Madame de Merteuil and Valmont to corrupt and confuse their correspondents, especially Cécile Volanges, Danceny, and the Présidente de Tourvel. In a letter to Cécile, Merteuil advises: "Take more care of your style.... You will agree, I am sure, that when you write to someone it is for his sake and not for yours. You must therefore try to say less what you think than what you think he will be pleased to hear" (CV, 252). Knowing *how* to write is as important as successfully transmitting the message, and this theme is an integral part of the motif of *epistolarity.*

The role of the reader, both real and fictional, also is essential to this motif. More perhaps than in any other form of fiction, the reader's presence, and, as we saw in Merteuil's advice above, his or her relationship to the writer, have an important effect on how one writes. Though chapter 4 of this study will discuss in depth the role reading plays in the *Liaisons,* perhaps a brief look at how it fits into the motif of *epistolarity* will be beneficial. "Every letter . . . is an exercise in rhetoric," says Duchêne (p. 74), and even a cursory reading of the popular manuals on how to write letters supports this observation. The letter is used to convince, to relate, to lie, and to confuse. It is a rhetorical device (despite the warnings of some early manualists not to make it so) which presupposes, even demands a reader. As Altman says in her essay on "the weight of the reader": "the epistolary experience . . . is a reciprocal one. . . . Epistolary writing, as distinguished from simple first-person writing, refracts events through not one but two prisms — that of reader as well as writer. We as external readers must always interpret a given letter in the light of its intended recipient" (pp. 113, 117).

There are several layers of readers involved in the creation of an epistolary work: the nonfictional reader (you and I), the fictitious "editor" or "rédacteur," the intended reader (the addressee), the "accidental" reader (anyone but the intended reader). All these readers help to create the novel from the series of fragments which an epistolary collection affords us — they help fill in the blank spaces which separate the letters. They criticize, misread (purposefully and mistakenly), misdirect, collect, order, and finally publish correspondences. And they are constant reminders that the letter is a dangerous, or at least very powerful instrument in the hands of a resourceful reader; therefore, one must write carefully and sparingly. We, the real readers, from our "privileged" and artificially neutral status, are asked to structure the apparent disorder of an epistolary novel, thereby imitating the fictional readers who also are trying to order their responses to the stimuli of separate and contradictory letters. How do we assign "meaning" to the collection? This is the ultimate question that the "real" reader should address, since the letter novelists of this period intuited, as one prominent critic is trying to teach us, that "literature is in the reader."[31]

Finally, some mention should be made, before leaving the analysis of this motif, of the strategies of storytelling, or novelmaking. The exchange of letters and the resultant transmission of information are integral to our subgenre, but the formulation of that information into a structured, comprehensible pattern must not be overlooked. When all the letters of the collection are ordered, edited, and published, we have the final product, which gives us, the non-fictional readers, a view of the correspondents' experience which they could not have had. The letter novel, with its apparently discrete narrative units, emphasizes one of the basic problems of all forms of fiction: how is a story told? In the present case, the individual letter writer chooses what he or she wants to tell or to emphasize; it is the "editor's" job to place those letters within a context, and to give them some order, thereby telling his or her own tale. Todorov chose to end his essay on Laclos with an observation on this point: "The history of the novel, the story of its creation, is found to be integrated into the very narrative structure of the novel.... Each work, each novel tells, through the texture of its events, the story of its own creation, tells its own story.... The meaning of a work consists in its own telling, in telling us of its own existence."[32] The result is a complex series of interferences on the level of creation, another characteristic of the epistolary novel. As Rousset has explained in his *Narcisse romancier:* "By committing narration to several functions, characters, different styles, the epistolary method constrains the narrative to be discontinuous; it fragments it, dispensing it among several editors who do not know its totality; only the book's reader is in a position to reconstruct it" (p. 21). And even this last statement is not absolutely valid; we know only what the "editor" wants to tell or give us.

The epistolary novel is a form fascinated with its own structure. It has the appearance of discontinuity, of disorder, of immediacy, of intimacy. As Richardson himself said: "I know not of any essential difference between this and any other way of writing novels, save only, that by making use of letters the writer is freed from the regular beginnings and conclusions of stories, with some other formalities, in which the reader of taste finds no less ease and advantage than the author himself."[33] And the preoccupations of a period such as the eighteenth century found such an apparent "formlessness" compatible. The open-endedness of the form underlined the increasingly emphasized open-mindedness and disparateness of human experience. In reference to another type of novel, the sentimental novel à la Sterne, Mackenzie, and Goethe, Leo Braudy makes some astute observations which could be profitably applied to epistolary fiction as well:

Ultimately the sentimental novel asserts the superiority of the inarticulate language of the heart to the artifice of literary and social forms, the articulate mind and the fluent pen.... In general, the sentimental novel opposes intuition to rationality; disjuncture, episode, and effusion to continuity and plot; artlessness and sincerity to art and literary calculation; and emotional to verbal communication.... The anti-literary pose of the sentimental novel is therefore neither naïve nor hypocritical nor some elaborate game designed to gull the reader, ... [but an attempt to develop] a kind of narrative that could preserve both formal elasticity and a constant relation between what was being told, and the act of telling.[34]

The artistic self-consciousness of the narrators in an epistolary work gives an extra dimension to the form and provides us not only with another defining motif but also closely ties this type of fiction to all fiction, giving us a perspective on the modern novel and its development which has heretofore been largely ignored.

VII *Conclusions*

The discussion of this last motif leads to a few concluding remarks on how this type of study can help one appreciate the place of such works as *Les Liaisons dangereuses* in the development of the modern novel. In an essay entitled "Towards a Poetics of Fiction,"[35] Barbara Hardy makes some observations about the making of narrative which are pertinent to the purposes of this essay. "...We go to novels to find out about narrative" (p. 5); eighteenth- and nineteenth-century novels, as would those of Joyce, Proust, and Beckett, tried to "represent the same confused and complex fluency of recording" that is narrative. "Narratives and dramas are often *about* making up stories and playing roles" (p. 7). This essay has shown how, though epistolary fiction had its problems (it was not the most felicitous of forms), letter novelists asked and wrestled with many of the bothersome questions of novel writing that would continue to haunt their successors. The motifs which I discussed, to repeat, were not meant to exclude any other possible motifs, nor were they meant to separate epistolary fiction from other types of narrative fiction. They do not define epistolary narrative alone; however, their redundant presence in the letter novel does lead to the following conclusions.

First, their determination permits us to talk coherently about an important literary subgenre, emphasizing its distinctive characteristics other than by referring to it as does a prominent literary handbook, as "a [type of] novel in which the narrative is carried forward by letters written by one or more of the characters." Also, letter fiction was a testing-ground for many serious questions concerning the craft of writing fiction, and, because of its peculiar structure, demanded the best efforts of the writers toward solving the problems of narrative point of view, temporal construction, thematic consistency, and character portrayal. Its historical moment was that of the appearance of what we refer to as the "modern" novel, and again, this fact alone makes it an important subgenre to understand. Finally, epistolary fiction is still the form to which many of those critics turn who are attempting to evolve theories of narratology that seek to reveal the modes of narrative discourse. (I think especially here of critics such as Rousset, Culler, Todorov, and Genette.) Increasingly, the genre is being seen, not as a clumsy response to what Georges May called the "dilemme du roman," but as an important advance in the history of narrative fiction.

The study of the epistolary novel provides us with a fascinating view of the creation and development of a literary subgenre. However, the motifs of *absence, time, exchange, reflexivity,* and *epistolarity* were not "chosen" by the letter novelists; they were imposed by the very nature of narrative fiction. The novelist's response to their demands led occasionally to formal and thematic dead ends, but eventually they formulated a nascent poetics of narrative fiction which is still being evolved today. It is incumbent on us as critics to isolate and teach those codes of fiction, not only to understand better the history of the novel, but other conceptual modes of human consciousness as well.

CHAPTER 4

Reading, Writing, and Meaning in Les Liaisons dangereuses

I *The Problematics of Reading*

W HAT is *Les Liaisons dangereuses* about? Does the knowledge of its story (its *histoire*) and of the generic tradition of which it is part make any clearer what Laclos wanted to impress on his readers? Does the way we read the novel help determine its meaning? Does Laclos impose any specific reading(s) on us? Is the reading of the novel problematic, and, if so, for what reasons? How does this problematic manifest itself? These questions will be tentatively answered in this chapter. Their analysis will provide an interpretive strategy for the appreciation and control, if only partial, of *Les Liaisons dangereuses*.

There is no need to list the dozens of articles and monographs that have attempted to discover the "real" meaning of Laclos's novel.[1] In fact, it is difficult to address the question without falling into the same hermeneutic trap, a tendency which is best acknowledged by this author before proceeding.[2] And yet this enormous critical apparatus would have pleased Laclos, for he sets the rules of the game *before* we read the first letter of the collection, and they are simple: read this novel, but at your own risk, for I have composed it in such a way as to thwart the methods of interpretation, developed through the reading of other novels, that you bring to the reading of this one. These "rules" are nowhere clearer than in the first two readings — one fictional, the other not — that we have of *Les Liaisons dangereuses*. The fictional one is found in the artfully juxtaposed "Publisher's Note" ("Avertissement de l'éditeur") and "Editor's Preface" ("Préface du rédacteur"), immediately preceding Letter I. These five pages (pp. 17–23 of the Penguin edition) raise and debate issues that were familiar to any intelligent reader of fiction in the second half of the eighteenth century.[3] The second, "nonfictional" reading was that performed by

Madame Riccoboni. Discussed in chapter 2 of the present study, it provides an excellent means by which to evaluate the ironical "prefaces" that precede the *Liaisons*. More will be said on this point below.

Laclos's putative publisher, sensing that he might have a best-seller on his hands, is careful to absolve himself of any charge of immorality, and so, superciliously warns "the over-credulous reader" in his one-page note: "We think it our duty to warn the public that, in spite of the title of this work and of what the editor says about it in his preface [which follows], we cannot guarantee its authenticity as a collection of letters: we have, in fact, very good reason to believe that it is *only a novel*" (p. 17, my italics). These final three words imply much more than a casual identification; a novel was not considered a "serious" genre; certainly it had a repu-tation for immorality, and its very naming tended simultaneously to titillate the reader while undermining any argument for moral verities that might be found in its pages. The fictitious publisher continues his preface by chiding Laclos for depicting contemporary French manners in such an unfavorable light. These events "must have happened in other places or at other times." Finally, as smug a critic as he is a moralist, the publisher concludes that the author has broken the most important rule that a novelist should follow, that of verisimilitude (*vraisemblance*): "We never see girls nowadays who have dowries of sixty thousand *livres* taking the veil, any more than we see young and pretty married women dying of grief." So there: fiction is debunked, morality is served, and the bourgeois publisher can go on to reap his rewards. This entry into the *Liai-sons* is a tricky one. Should "the over-credulous reader" accept the publisher's admonition that this work is a novel, then it is an "unrealistic" one, both artistically as well as morally, and there-fore not worthy of serious attention. Should he reject this view, and approach the work as an actual collection of letters, then he has at least been warned by the pious publisher, and in fact has been tantalized by the promise that he will find "characters . . . of such vicious habits that it is impossible to suppose they can have lived in our age."

Turning the page, the now-more-than-ever curious reader looks to the "editor" to straighten matters out, and to tell him if he is reading a novel or not, and, if so, if it will be harmful to the pub-lic's morals. From the beginning, though, things are unclear. The editor refers to "this work (*ouvrage*), or rather this collection of letters." He goes on to reveal that the collection "contains . . . only a very small portion of the correspondence from which it was drawn," that he has "set them [the letters] in order," and has tried "to retain only those letters which appeared necessary either to an understanding of events or to the development of the characters" (p. 19). So, within the first few lines of his preface, the "editor" has neutralized the ambiguity of the "publisher's" preface: even if the letters were real, he has so organized, collated, and edited them as to have formed his own version (his own "novel") of the events. He has been the arbiter of coherence and value; he has abridged and commented on (in about fifty footnotes) this "work" and will stand by its obvious merits. There follows a carefully contrived request addressed to the "reasonable" reader, the intelligent reader, the reader with good taste, to appreciate the difficulty of the editor's task and the earnestness of his achievement.

Most of the preface is taken up with an "answer" to the "publisher's" moral objections to the novel. The "editor" cagily selects his audience: "Those . . . who, before they begin to read a book, would be glad to know what, more or less, they are to expect, would do well to read on: others would do better to proceed immediately to the text itself. They know enough about it already" (p. 20). The temptation is to strike out on one's own, refusing any guides to or aid with the "reading" of the novel; but how many do so? There follows a well-argued justification for the publishing of this collection (and therefore for the specific "reading" given the original collection by the "editor"). The book can provide a certain type of "pleasure" (*agrément*), due to the variety of its styles and observations. Curiosity will guide the reader, "since nearly all the sentiments expressed are either pretended or dissembled" (pp. 20–21), another prejudgment that further restricts the reader's interpretive possibilities. But, in the end, "this collection can please very few"; neither libertines, nor freethinkers, nor the virtuous, nor the "fastidious" reader will enjoy it. Even "the general run of readers [*le commun des lecteurs*], misled by the idea that everything that is printed is the result of deliberation, will think they detect in [some letters] the laboured manner of an author who appears in person behind the characters through whom he speaks" (p. 22). Asks Laclos's reader: which of these types am I? Do I believe that this collection is real or not? Does it matter? The editor says that an "author" would have been overly concerned with the letters' style, depriving them of grace; however, printing them makes the letters' casual negligence even more glaring. Again, the reader of the *Liaisons* queries: Which did he do? How will I read this collection of letters? As fiction, nonfiction, or both?

There is little doubt that Laclos, through the already discussed strategy of juxtaposition, opened his novel with this "battle of the prefaces" in order to introduce a problematics of reading as one of the cohering structures of *Les Liaisons dangereuses*. It is difficult to write pertinently about this novel without writing about the role of reading — though most critics have tried. As explained in chapter 3, reading is an integral motif of letter fiction. The letter presupposes a reader; the letter novel presupposes that people know how to write and to read letters. T. Todorov and others have succeeded in making us aware of this fact, namely, that the *Liaisons* is as much a novel about novelmaking (and reading) as it is about anything else.[4] The novel "naturalizes," makes conventional the act of reading since that activity is integral to any novel's plot, character development and thematic cohesiveness. I have argued elsewhere that this was not an isolated phenomenon, that in fact "reading and novelmaking" were inextricably — and causally — linked.[5] There was an uncertainty about the constituency of one's readership, and novelists felt, as a result, the need to invent and persuade a readership for their works. The "modern novel," quite simply, appeared before its audience was defined. An analysis of fifty years of novel production, from Marivaux in the 1730s to Laclos in the 1780s, reveals a marked concern on the part of the best of these writers (including Diderot and Rousseau) to define their readership. Diderot's commentaries on *La Religieuse* and Richardson, and Rousseau's preface to *Julie, ou La Nouvelle Héloïse* are key texts in the development of a poetics of reading. Also, Laclos's comments on his public were not limited to two fictitious prefaces: in his essay on Burney's *Cecilia* as well as in his comments on Lacretelle's *Fils naturel,* he had insisted on the French reader's interest in events (*événements*) rather than characters, in the organization of the story first, the characters' reactions second (see, for example, Allem, p. 504).

Les Liaisons dangereuses was as well part of another tradition that put great emphasis on perception and control: the libertine novel. An active role played by the reader is essential to the successful creation of an erotic landscape. As Sade would show, understanding can be effected through the transfer of the erotic expectations of the reader to an epistemological level. In other words, the erotic impulse can be transposed, and thereby transformed, to a different plane of apprehension and interpretation. This process of disorientation succeeded in weakening one of the essential components of narrative theory in the eighteenth-century — that of verisimilitude (*vraisemblance*) — thereby disengaging narrative fiction from a tradition that had led it down many theoretical culs-de-sac. The mechanisms of eroticism (perfected by Sade, but employed by every successful novelist of the period) were used to eroticize the aesthetic quality of a text, thereby causing the reader to expect and receive pleasure from the hermeneutic process. *Les Liaisons dangereuses* is not a casually libertine novel, but a purposefully erotic one, arousing and utilizing the reader's most basic emotions in order to effect the most successful reading.

Given these contexts, it is no wonder that Laclos paid special attention to Madame Riccoboni's criticisms — the first extensive critique we have of the *Liaisons* — in her letters to him soon after the novel's appearance. However, an ironic reading of that correspondence emerges when one realizes that Madame Riccoboni uses the same arguments, even the same vocabulary of Laclos's fictitious "publisher." How unfortunate to use such obvious talents to paint customs that have never existed in France, she opines. "So much depravity is an irritant and fails to instruct" (Allem, p. 693); especially degrading is the portrait of French womanhood. Laclos's responses are subtle — as if he were unsure whether or not to take his fellow novelist's criticism seriously — and they emphasize the role that fiction must assume in order to examine those aspects of social organization and conventions unanalyzable by more traditional methods of inquiry. Like the Bishop of Pavia, who would ask Laclos for a copy of his novel years later because he had heard that it was a "moral" work, Madame Riccoboni had missed the point, had not accepted the rules of Laclos's novel. She refused to accept the problematic scheme set down in the prefaces, and the result was a "misreading," or, at best, an incomplete reading of the *Liaisons*.

Before proceeding with a discussion of "readings" of the *Liaisons,* it would perhaps be useful to some readers to present a brief survey of what has come to be called "the poetics of reading." Two critics have been most successful in delineating and applying such a "poetics" to the study of narrative fiction: Roland Barthes and Jonathan Culler.[6] Both critics define narrative fiction in terms of the reading strategies such works provide or frustrate. They reduce all the traditional categories of the criticism of fiction — plot, character, tone, point of view, and so forth — to categories based on a reading model.

Some of the tenets of this model, in summary and therefore lacking these critics' subtlety, reflect directly on the study of *Les Liaisons dangereuses*. They include the following propositions: (1) that the "best" texts provide a plurality of "meanings," with no hierarchy of values; (2) that, as a consequence, there can be no "correct" or "total reading" of a text since writing does not necessarily have a teleological aim; (3) that "reading" is not only a sequential, syntagmatic organization of data, but a process of reordering and readjustment which calls into play processes of paradigmatic substitution that involve as well as result from rereading, reading episodes (or letters) out of sequence, skimming, and so forth;[7] (4) that readings are differential, that is, their strategies result from a combination of "literary competence" (what the reader brings to the text) and authorial manipulation or directives; (5) that the most important function of narrative fiction is the production of plausible models of interpretation, to be applied to life experiences, that can be rejected, accepted or modified by the reader; (6) that the concept of the "reader" is a methodological construct which can be applied to any number of hypostatized subjects: the historical author, the fictional author, various (or all) characters, the "real" reader, and so forth; and, finally, (7) that when completed, a poetics of reading should have addressed and isolated the problem of *what* exactly is needed in order to read appropriately (economically and efficiently), that is, how to identify conventions and/or rules that a culture imposes on a text.

Laclos's awareness of the complex motivations and processes of reading a novel, especially a letter novel, pervades his text. One might hesitate to place him in the vanguard of those who — beginning with Flaubert — would seek, as Culler has argued in his important study of that nineteenth-century novelist, "to dislocate the process of communication in which readers would attempt to participate, [thereby] creating problems of interpretation."[8] Laclos was a derivative thinker, and considerably less critical (as his occasional writings indicate) of the theoretical traditions that formed him than other writers who had preceded him; yet, he was a very good reader himself, steeped in a rich education gleaned from seventeenth- and eighteenth-century fiction, and obviously aware of the problematic nature, on both an ethical and aesthetic level, of fictional literature.

To return to the question that opened this chapter — what is *Les Liaisons dangereuses* about? — we can, in the context of the previous discussion, reach a tentative conclusion. The *Liaisons* is "about" those subjects that most critics have agreed on: social morality and ethics, their rules and transgressions, class structures and their interaction, the organization and transgression of cultural systems (for example, religious and political organization, methods of colecting and diffusing information), and the economics of sexual as well as intellectual desire. But, in addition, the *Liaisons* is a novel that addresses the problem of interpreting and communicating these various phenomena. It is a self-conscious work that, through a "play of mirrors," imposes a spiraling strategy of reading that results in only one certainty: the absence of certainty. This concept of reading is thematized in various ways by Laclos, and a series of examples should reveal how pervasive the problematic is as well as how it places into question writing, a corollary of reading.

II   *The Thematics of Reading and Writing*

We have seen how the "battle of the prefaces" thematizes the problem of reading from the first page of *Les Liaisons dangereuses*. Examples will be given below of how the process of reading is also thematized by the novel's major correspondents in such a way as to become a metaphor for other means of interpreting the signs of social behavior, and not only linguistic ones. However, we should pause briefly in our analysis of the problematics and thematics of reading to examine its corollary of writing. To state the obvious, reading presupposes writing; a letter does not in effect fulfill its function until and unless it is read, but it has to be written first. The exchange of letters can be compared to the dialogic process of communication. However, unlike oral dialogue, either face-to-face, or, in modern times, by telephone or radio, written dialogue is temporally disjunctive. It is impossible — or at least highly improbable — that a letter can be read simultaneously with its writing. So, as we emphasized in chapter 3, a letter implies from its inception the need to compensate for an absence. It attempts to fill a perceived void.

But there is a more important distinction to be made between oral and written dialogue, and that has to do with the permanency of the written word. Every correspondent makes a commitment to permanency — wittingly or not — when he or she puts ink or pencil on paper. The intent, then, of the dialogic process is potentially perverted, for, no matter what the initial reason for the letter, it can be read, reread, misread, misinterpreted at will, long after the event for which it was originally written has passed. It becomes a record, losing with time its dialogic aspect. Tourvel, Merteuil, and Valmont are acutely conscious of this possibility. We learn in Letter 44 that Tourvel has kept copies of the originals of all of Valmont's letters, most likely so as to be able to trade with him should ever her demand for the return of her own be met. In fact, she agrees, fatefully, to meet with him in Paris, ostensibly to ensure "the return of my letters, which he has kept till now in spite of my request to the contrary" (CXXIV, 292). As early as Letter 78, she had expressed concern about the image people would have of her if they read Valmont's letters to her: "Anyone reading your letters would think me either unjust or very strange" (p. 167), because they would be read out of context. Merteuil, in several places, mentions the danger of leaving letters lying around. After Madame de Volanges discovered (at Merteuil's direction) Danceny's letters to Cécile, Merteuil writes Valmont: "I think I have taught her [Cécile] so severe a lesson on the danger of keeping letters that I may venture now to write to her myself" (LXIII, 138). And, later in Letters 81 and 85, she avers that she never writes letters (except to Valmont) and burns immediately those she receives (both observations made unintentionally ironic by the very fact that we are reading them). Finally, Valmont shows that he too is aware of how letters can be misconstrued, observing at one point to Merteuil that a judicious editing of her correspondence could make Cécile look guiltier than she was: "A carefully chosen selection of these letters would show that the little Volanges had made all the advances and indeed thrown herself at [Danceny's] head" (LXVI, 144).

Besides being potentially dangerous, letterwriting is seen as only partially successful as a means of seduction by Merteuil and Valmont. Again, they emphasize the need for face-to-face dialogue (and, after all, is not their aim to attain the ultimate physical contact?). Written words lack the subtlety that spoken language, combined with gesture, intonation, and physical emotion, can impart. This is one of the novel's most insidious themes, namely, that writing is less "good," less honest, more dangerous than the directness of oral dialogue.[9] Merteuil, in a very important letter to Valmont (Letter 33), warns him of the inefficiency of letterwriting in matters of seduction:

> Your real mistake is in allowing yourself to enter into a correspondence. I defy you to foresee where this will lead you.... Consider how long it takes to write a letter, how long it takes getting it delivered, and tell me whether any woman of principle such as your Fair Devotee [Tourvel], could possibly sustain for that length of time an intention she struggles constantly to suppress.... *She is more than your match in letter-writing.* (p. 79, italics mine)

There follows a lengthy passage on the primacy of "conversation" (oral communication) over writing, for matters of seduction, implying, that for any successful venture requiring communication between two parties, oral is "better" than written language, presence more effective than absence. The passion of the writer, real to him, is mediated and thereby weakened by the written word:

> There is not the same difficulty in conversation. Long practice in using the voice has made it a sensitive instrument; tears that come easily are an added advantage; and in the eyes an expression of desire is not easily distinguished from tenderness. Moreover it is easier, in the informality of conversation, to achieve that excitement and incoherence which is the true eloquence of love. Above all, the presence of the beloved is a check to thought and an incentive to surrender. (p. 79)

This passage — in fact, the whole letter — underscores one of the novel's least-analyzed themes: the perception of the insufficiency, on an ethical and aesthetic plane, of communicational codes in a highly developed culture. Writing is simply seen by all concerned in this work as insufficient, unclear, misleading, ineffective, and generally inferior to direct, oral communication. Says Danceny, in a letter to Merteuil: "What can one say in a letter which a word, a look, or even a silence could not express a hundred times better?" (CL, 351). The protocol of epistolary correspondence has succeeded in devaluating written language to such an extent that, in order to counteract its effects, *more* has to be written. The system is not an economical one: the more that is written, the more one needs to clarify, and the more vulnerable one becomes as his or her letters leave traces and records for others to find and interpret.

If writing, then, is thematized in *Les Liaisons dangereuses* in such a way as to make it suspect, then how is reading thematized? The answer, though obvious, is difficult to summarize since the theme permeates the novel. We have seen in the previous chapter how the self-conscious motif of *epistolarity* is essential to letter fiction. Laclos refines this motif and uses it not only for reasons of verisimilitude but as an autocriticism as well. In other words, Laclos never allows his readers to forget that they are *reading,* and that reading is not a neutral activity. His characters, like us, are exegetes; they read and reread their own letters and letters of others. They need to read, and to be read, and while performing this activity are led to reflect on it. The *activity of reading* is clearly emphasized by the novel's correspondents. For instance, in Letter 150, Danceny uses the metaphor of a portrait to make clearer a *sine qua non* of epistolary knowledge: letters unread, though important signs, have the same deceptive promise of immediacy as a portrait. He is writing to Merteuil about the pain of his future separation from her: "...However long our time together, it must end in separation: and then one is so alone! It is then that a letter is precious! If one does not read it, one may at least look at it.... Ah, yes: one may certainly look at a letter without reading it, just as, it seems to me, I can still find pleasure in touching your portrait at night...." (p. 352). These comments, perhaps unwittingly, draw attention to a point that is obvious, yet so often understated, namely, that a letter, like a portrait, is a *sign* of absence; however, *reading* that letter adds an almost palpable dimension to the absent correspondent. In other words, reading makes real; failing to read leaves the sign unfulfilled.

As pointed out earlier, the first "reader" of the *Liaisons* was the so-called "editor," he who was asked by the Rosemonde family to compose an edition of the extant correspondence. His presence is felt throughout the collection in two ways, one subtle, the other blatant. The first has to do with his juxtaposition of the letters of the various correspondents. There is no more subtle manipulation of the extratextual reader than this mechanism. Ostensibly, he orders the letters chronologically, but since the time span of the novel is only a few months, and since many of the letters are written on the same day by different correspondents, such a model for ordering is soon insufficient.[10] He proceeds then "to set them in order" (p. 19) according to his own reading. The result is, as Laclos's title implies, a dangerous series of juxtapositions, yet a challenge to us to reread them in any order we might wish. Not unlike efforts by contemporary writers, such as Julio Cortázar in his *Hopscotch,* to effect different strategies of sequential reading, Laclos seems to welcome similar efforts from those who have read his novel for the first time to pick it up again to see how they were manipulated. *Les Liaisons dangereuses,* more than any other novel of the *ancien régime* (except perhaps for Diderot's *La Religieuse*), demands a second reading immediately following the first.

However, to return to the editor's juxtaposition of the letters, from the beginning of the novel, with its eye-opening conjunction of Cécile's and Merteuil's letters, the reader is sensitized to the possibility that meaning is as often produced by a sequential ordering as by the letters themselves. (It is no wonder that modern structuralist criticism has been so fascinated with the example of the *Liaisons:* significance more often than not devolves from the differences between these signs rather than from their individual content.) Besides juxtaposing letters from different correspondents, the "editor" can also provide a sequence of letters by the same writer to different persons. One such sequence — Letters 104–106 — written by Merteuil is especially exemplary. Letter 104 is a reply to Madame de Volanges who has asked for Merteuil's help in dealing with her daughter's affair with Danceny; Letter 105 is to Cécile, pledging help in deceiving her now vigilant mother; and Letter 106 is to Valmont, commenting on his activities as well as on the two previous letters. Such a juxtaposition comes too late in the novel to reveal anything we, as readers, have not already divined about Merteuil's manipulative subterfuges; however, it serves as a timely reminder that such strategic juxtapositions are occurring constantly, though perhaps less blatantly, and that the reader should be on guard. Allowing himself to skim, to be overcome by the ever present though unsuspected power of boredom, the reader can find himself soon manipulated as often and as humiliatingly as Cécile was.

The "editor's" job of organization is duplicated at least twice by Valmont, who sends Merteuil packets of letters with careful instructions on the order in which they should be read. They concern the following sequences: Letters 34, 35, 36, and Letters 40, 41, 42. In the first, Valmont supplements his recapitulation of events with drafts of two letters between him and Tourvel, advising Merteuil to read his first, then his victim's response. In the second sequence, Valmont interrupts his Letter 40 in this way: "As soon as we reached the house she went up to her room, while I retired to

mine to read the epistle which you, too, would do well to read —
and my reply to it — before proceeding further..." (p. 94). Letter
40 takes up again after Merteuil (and we) would have read the other
two. There are other such sequences in the novel: letters enclosed
with other letters, directives for reading that left the putative "editor" little choice in his ordering. But, in the main, the correspondence, as we have it, is supposed to be the result of one man's
"reading" — his culling, editing, arranging — and his presence is
constantly felt.

The second, less subtle manner by which the "editor" is perceived is through his use of footnotes. There are about fifty such
notes in the novel, occurring at regular intervals, with the longest
interval between notes never being more than fifteen or so letters
(in fact, intervals of more than five letters without a note occur
only four times in the novel). Study of the manuscript preserved in
the Bibliothèque Nationale and of subsequent editions of the *Liaisons* give proof to the idea that Laclos considered these notes of
sufficient value to correct and change them.[11] The footnotes,
marked by asterisks in the manuscript and most editions, fall into
several categories, all of which can be considered as directives for a
reading of the letters or sequence to which they are attached.

The first type is explanatory of names referring to persons,
places, or things outside the immediate world of the novel, for
example, Letter 1: "a fellow-pupil" (p. 23); Letter 85: "Some
readers may not, perhaps, be aware that a *macédoine* is a medley of
several games of chance..." (p. 202); Letter 101: "A village half-
way between Paris and Madame de Rosemonde's château"
(p. 240). These notes give an aura of verisimilitude to the letters, as
well as a certain palpability to the "editor," who obviously knows
the society and circumstances depicted by the letters.

The second type are cross-referential, that is, they refer to other
letters in the collection. For example, Letter 81: "In a subsequent
letter (152) the reader will learn, not Monsieur de Valmont's secret,
but the nature of it..., and will appreciate why it was not possible
to enter here into fuller explanations on the subject" (p. 186);
Letter 85: "See Letter 74" (p. 195); Letter 125: "Letters 120 and
122" (p. 297). Also, several references are made to lost letters.
Such cross-references again underscore the fact that this collection
has already been read, and remind the reader that he will need all of
his mnemonic powers to keep track of the correspondents' references and commentary.

The third category of notes might be called literary. References are simple, mentioning only the name of an author or work (for example, "Rousseau," "*Nouvelle Héloïse,*" "Voltaire, *Nanine*") referred to in the text of the letter (see Letters 4, 44, 63, 99, 110 for examples). The "editor," then, is a scholar, as well-read as the correspondents. Also, references to such a novelist as Rousseau emphasize the fictional nature of this correspondence, as well as the source of much of the sentimental education of the protagonists.

Fourth, we have a series of footnotes that comment on the motivations of some of the correspondents, pass judgment on their styles, and so forth. This category, and the following one, are the most manipulative, and the most significant in terms of effecting a certain reading of the letters. They challenge the reader: either accept my evaluation, or else make a valid one on your own. In the present category, examples may be found in Letter 9: "Madame de Volanges' mistake shows that, like all other rogues, Valmont never betrayed his accomplices" (p. 38); Letter 65: "Monsieur Danceny's admisions are not altogether honest" (p. 142); and Letter 81: "Being an occasional reader of poetry, [Monsieur Danceny's] more practised ear helped him to avoid errors of taste" (p. 180).

The final category, mixed in carefully with the more traditional explanatory notes of the other types, is "self-referential," dealing with the *task of editing* and thereby of interpreting the correspondence. As early as Letter 7, a lengthy note explains:

> So as not to try the patience of the reader, a large part of the daily correspondence between these young ladies has been suppressed. Only those letters appear which are necessary to an understanding of the course of events. For the same reason all Sophie Carnay's letters, and several written by others who figure in this history, have been omitted. (p. 35)

Such reminders recur: Letter 39: "Letters between Cécile Volanges and the Chevalier Danceny continue to be omitted since they are of little interest and throw no light on events" (p. 92); Letter 61: "The letter from Cécile Volanges to the Marquise has been omitted as containing no more than the facts presented above with fewer details" (p. 131). One note in Letter 169, from Danceny to Madame de Rosemonde, refers back to the preface, reminding the reader of the correspondence's provenance: "It is from this collection of letters, from the one that was delivered into the same hands at the death of Madame de Tourvel and from certain letters entrusted, also to Madame de Rosemonde, by Madame de Volanges, that the present collection has been formed. The originals remain in the hands of Madame de Rosemonde's heirs" (p. 380).

But, the two most important notes of this type are those that appear in Letter 154 and in Letter 175, the last of the novel. The first is misleadingly simple. Madame de Volanges writes to Madame de Rosemonde that she cannot fathom a letter written to her by Valmont about Tourvel: "But I wonder," she writes in the letter, "what you will say to this despair of Monsieur de Valmont's. In the first place, is one to believe him, or does he want only to deceive us all, even to the last?" Here, the note is placed; it reads: "It was because nothing was found in the ensuing correspondence to resolve this doubt, that it was decided to suppress Monsieur de Valmont's letter" (p. 359). Laclos had written such a letter (it can be found in the appendix of the Penguin edition, pp. 394-95), so why did he remove it and replace it with a note? Part of the answer is that Laclos wanted to make his reader aware of the "editor's" discretionary presence. The editor is saying that the reader cannot be trusted in this case, as he has been in numerous others, to make any more of a valid judgment than Madame de Volanges had. Valmont's letter, say both the "editor" and Laclos, might have confused the reader to such an extent that the rhythm of the last twenty-five letters of the correspondence would be interrupted. Still, the reason for this note remains obscure unless we accept the interpretation that Laclos thought the evolution of Valmont's character could be more effectively described by those who write to and about him than by himself.

The last note, in Letter 175, brings us full circle back to the prefaces. However, this note is not written by the "editor," but by the "publisher." It assumes the same tone of moral superiority found in the first preface, and the reader is left once again in limbo about how to interpret the novel's "moral." The most lengthy of the footnotes, it not only explains why the correspondence must end here, but it evaluates the readers' putative response to the whole collection:

For motives of our own — and certain other considerations which we shall always consider it our duty to respect — we are compelled to stop here.

We can, at the present moment, give the reader neither the subsequent adventures of Mademoiselle de Volanges, nor any account of the sinister occurrences which crowned the misfortunes and accomplished the punishment of Madame de Merteuil.

Some day, perhaps, we shall be permitted to complete this work. But we cannot commit ourselves on this point: and if it were possible, we should still think ourselves obligated in the first place to consult the public taste, since the public and we have not the same motives [*raisons*] for being interested in the book. (p. 393)

This sudden and final ravishment of the text from the more sophisticated and subtle "editor" jolts the reader. Is there any more to the story? What else did happen to Merteuil? What does he mean that my "motives" are different from his? Have I not read this story the way it should be read? Such questions are intentionally raised by these final comments, and bring the reader back to the question that opened this chapter: what is *Les Liaisons dangereuses* about? The question, as we shall see in the final section of this essay, is left hanging by this obnoxious note. Through his scarce but regular use of annotation, Laclos directs our attention to several persistent concerns of his fictional correspondents: how to read, how not to misread, how to avoid being misread, how to reread, and so forth.

There are a few other manifestations of this phenomenon that deserve brief attention. *Les Liaisons dangereuses* is replete with directives for interpretation. Each correspondent shows that he or she is a careful reader by making exact reference to his or her correspondent's own text (for example, Letters 10, 26, 35, 56, 63). The hermeneutic impulse, with its infinite possibilities for misapprehension, is strong in Laclos's letters. Also, as mentioned above in reference to the "literary category" of notes, Laclos reminds us that his characters did not read only their letters but other things as well. Merteuil, awaiting a lover, reads "a chapter of *Le Sopha* [by Crébillon *fils*], a letter from [Rousseau's] *Héloïse,* and two of La Fontaine's tales, so as to establish in my mind the different nuances of tone I wished to adopt" (X, 42). Later, Cécile writes in Letter 29 that Merteuil would give her books in which she could learn how to write. Perhaps the most important passage concerning the reading of other books in the *Liaisons* occurs in Merteuil's autobiographical Letter 81: "I supplemented [my observations] with the aid of books [*la lecture*]: and they were not all the kind you imagine. I studied our manners in the novelists, our opinions in the philosophers; I went to the strictest moralists to find out what they demanded of us, so as to know for certain what it was possible to do, what it was best to think, and what it was necessary to seem to be" (p. 184). A final example of this mania for therapeutic reading occurs when Tourvel, at her wit's end over how to handle the importunings of Valmont, retires to her room, taking two books from Madame de Rosemonde's library to console her: "the second volume of *Christian Thoughts,* [and] the first volume of a book entitled *Clarissa*" (CVII, 257). These are the most revealing of numerous references to reading as a source of knowledge and comfort, references that support the motif of *reflexivity* that underlies this entire novel.

Laclos wanted his reader to feel ambiguous about reading *Les Liaisons dangereuses,* about its language and its subject matter. There is no other explanation for the constant play, through juxtaposition and cross-reference, around the idea of reading and interpreting. On one hand, the reader cannot help but "interpret" whenever he finds a discrepancy; on the other, every time he "interprets," he runs the risk of being "wrong," and thereby of losing self-confidence in his talents as a good reader. Early in the novel, in Letter 48, Valmont, a great punster and master of the *double-entendre,*[12] writes the letter which is one of the two best-known in the collection (the other being Letter 81). This missive, addressed to Tourvel, and intended to show Merteuil that he is *not* in love with the Présidente, is written while he is in bed, making love to a courtesan, Emilie. The letter mocks the vocabulary of love, epistolary protocol, and his pretended affections for Tourvel. Yet, had we not known that Emilie was lying beside him, the following line would have been read entirely differently, as it was by the unsuspecting Tourvel: "... I must leave you for a moment to calm an excitement which mounts with every moment, and which is fast becoming more than I can control" (p. 111). This is a blatant example of *double-entendre,* amusing and well-done; it demands a rereading, and maybe even a third reading, at first to laugh, and then to wonder. If such circumstances help interpret a letter that can be totally misread by its intended recipient, then what circumstances determine the reading (and "interpretation") of the other letters written by Valmont and Merteuil? This unsubtle technique is used rarely by Laclos, but enough to make us question, and ideally to reread the other letters written by his two roguish protagonists.

The thematics of reading and writing in *Les Liaisons dangereuses* are tantalizing and frustrating. They lead the reader toward one of

Laclos's most problematic subjects, that of "meaning," and lead him there using all the subtlety and power of a tradition that few other novelists have manipulated so well. If Laclos's novel is "about" meaning, it is also "about" tradition: its forms, its excuses and justifications, its dangers and enticements. None of the characters in *Les Liaisons dangereuses* can escape the formative power of cultural codes. They try to; they even deceive themselves into believing they succeed, but, in the end, they have only done what Laclos lures us into doing: they have misread.

III   *The Lure of Meaning*

"This collection can please very few," says its "editor" (p. 22). He is speaking about its moral ambiguities, but the same can be said for its resistance to the assignation of meaning in a more general sense. The two prefaces prevent a certain approach, but simultaneously tempt the reader — especially the reader of other eighteenth-century fiction — to discover the reasons for the novel's composition, its didactic message. Laclos, in a strikingly modern way, seeks to undercut the evolved procedures by which readers assign meaning to fiction, in this case, an epistolary novel.

The first letter of the collection is more than a vehicle to introduce Cécile, the victim. It also metaphorizes both the act of reading and the act of assigning meaning. Cécile is writing an enthusiastic letter to her friend Sophie Carnay, who is still at the convent where both girls had been boarded and schooled. She is excited about being at home, in her own room, with her own servants, and with her mother, who has become her friend and her confidant. She knows that she is to be married, but not to whom or when. As she writes, someone drives up in a carriage, is announced, and Cécile, believing this arrival to be her intended, drops her pen and rushes downstairs. On her return to her desk, she confides to Sophie that she has just made a fool of herself:

> As I came into Mamma's room I saw, standing by her, a gentleman dressed in black. I greeted him as best I could and stood there, quite unable to move. You can imagine how I scrutinized him!
> "Madame," he said to my mother as he bowed to me. "What a charming young lady; I am more than ever sensible to the extent of your kindness."
> The meaning of this was so plain that I was seized with trembling and

my knees gave way; I found a chair and sat down, very flushed and very disconcerted. I had hardly done this when the man was at my feet. Upon which I lost my head; I was, as Mamma said, utterly panic-stricken. I jumped up uttering a piercing shriek ... just as I did that day there was a thunderstorm, do you remember? Mamma burst out laughing, and said: "Come now, what is the matter? Sit down and give your foot to Monsieur." In short, my dear, the gentleman was a shoemaker. (p. 24)

I cite this passage at length, not solely because it is an amusing anecdote, but because Laclos chooses to begin his novel with the very question: what does all this mean? The reader scarcely guesses that the man in black is a shoe salesman before Cécile does. She wants to surprise her friend with the anecdote's ending, and, in turn, we are surprised as well. Laclos will leave more subtle indications in the early part of his novel, but his warning is clear: before you arrive at any conclusions, remember that no narrator can be trusted; they are either naive, or blind, or duplicitous, or occasionally all three. And yet, every impulse of tradition has conditioned the reader to discover some stable level of interpretation that will allow him to organize the bits of data that these dangerous letters represent. There is a lure of meaning, at once used and rejected by Laclos, and this process of temptation and frustration within the context of the production of meaning is an essential intrigue of *Les Liaisons dangereuses*.

Laclos was a man who was attracted to, and repulsed by, tradition. The story of his life is the story of a man who tries to make it within systems (military, social, literary, political), while fighting the system at the same time. He was a writer at the end of a long tradition of other novelists who had attempted to map out an area of investigation and structures for effecting those investigations, and he worked within that tradition. However, as we have seen in this chapter, he questioned most of these previous assumptions in an original and, ultimately, deconstructive way. Reading, he seems to say, provides a means for uncovering the cognitive processes exposed through writing. Yet, since writing is essentially a perversion of the communicative act, an activity at the base of which is a desire to deceive, then reading, a corollary of writing, is likewise an activity based on a false premise. Neither of these activities can provide an ideal meaning, a final version, a resolution of ambiguous signals and equally attractive though paradoxical messages. As we discovered in chapter 2, the context defines any meaning-producing activity, and the variability and impermanence of contexts thereby destabilize any attempts at discovering an immutable meaning.

Another process of destabilization takes place as well. The reader(s) of these texts are never allowed to assume any status of privileged observation. We have seen repeatedly how all of the major correspondents of the *Liaisons* reflect our own tendencies to misread. Laclos's brilliant juxtaposition and ordering of letters, his manipulation of the temporal aspects of the collection, his emphasis on the devaluation of the vocabulary of *sensibilité* (especially in the letters of Merteuil and Valmont), his use of anecdotes and apparently extraneous episodes: all these strategies succeed in disrupting the signifying processes of the reader (the "subject"). This process of destabilization is more than a sophisticated game of literary dynamics. Laclos is questioning the value of some of the Enlightenment's most cherished assumptions. Taking a page from Rousseau's book, Laclos directs his novel not toward the effete, smug aristo-bourgeois society that he was trying, in part, to impress, but toward the purportedly worthy successors to the great Enlighteners, using the myths of the Enlightenment as tools and a context to criticize those who wished to continue it.

In his study of Flaubert, Jonathan Culler outlines the procedure through which "the readers are to be demoralized" in order to make them more reflective about their present condition. (Culler is speaking here of Flaubert's utilization of, and response to, Romantic irony, but his comments, I think, are equally relevant to any novelist's use of irony as a critique of cultural assumptions.) "Three things must be done," he argues, "which though inseparable in the final achievement might well have failed independently of one another.... There must be, first of all, a compulsion to identify the text with a world conventionally regarded as real." Laclos adroitly manipulates this process of identification through the "publisher's" assurance that nothing could be further from the truth than the assumptions of this novel's "plot." Equally important, continues Culler, "and this is again a device for the creation of objectivity, the language of the text must be isolated from any definable narrator, and this is perhaps most easily done through irony." Laclos uses as well the awkward first-person, epistolary format to disperse the narrative personae and to frustrate any attempt to create an independent, definable narrating persona. (The extratextual manifestation of this phenomenon is discussed in chapter 6.) The ultimate ironic comment is that the form Laclos chose is, on a referential level, an absolute sign for communication, yet, as he illustrates repeatedly, it is inefficient and insufficient. Last, "and perhaps most importantly, demoralization is produced by undermining the conventions of reading, hampering the operations which readers are accustomed to perform on texts so as to 'make sense' of them, but hampering these operations with sufficient subtlety that readers will not throw down the books in a moment of frustration."[13] I trust that the previous discussion has indicated how Laclos fulfills this last requirement for writing a "modern" text.

Too close to the tradition he wanted to ironize, too much dependent on the vagaries of public taste and publication demands, Laclos would not attain the level of distinction of Flaubert. He was, for the most part, unable to break away from the metaphysical underpinnings of his cultural traditions. He perceived, less subtly and less originally than Rousseau had, but accurately, that the informational aspects of artistic expression were proving to be insufficient to deal with the increasing complexity of a culture reaping the benefits of a revolution in scientific, historiographical, and philosophic inquiry. It should not be forgotten that Laclos himself was a trained engineer and an original military inventor; the facility with which he moved between the aesthetic domain and the scientific one implies as well a belief in the reciprocal, unified nature of human inquiry. Nonetheless, though he perceived deficiencies in language and other manners of expression, he was not original enough to transcend these paradoxes in order to deal with them on another, superior level. And yet, his perception of them was therapeutic, for himself and, eventually, for his readers. *Les Liaisons dangereuses* is one of those important texts that question other texts; it is a self-conscious reading of cultural stereotypes intended to question — and occasionally to support — those stereotypes.

In more ways than one, Laclos was an apt pupil of Rousseau, his hero, for Jean-Jacques had, more brilliantly than any of his contemporaries, realized and developed the notion that language was an "unnatural" invention that separated man from his "natural" state, preventing him from discovering his origins. Whether, as contemporary philosophical investigations in France have suggested, this was a form of metaphysical blindness and self-deception is not essential here. What is important is that Laclos was not unaware of the two dominant legacies of the Enlightenment — language as control and language as nemesis — and he opted for one, the latter, over the other, thereby forming an important link between the Enlightenment and Romanticism.

If there is an answer to our insistent question — what is *Les Liaisons dangereuses* about? — it has to be somewhat different from what we have come to expect in terms of discovering a "meaning." In the case of this novel, we might change slightly our use of the term "meaning," emphasize its participle quality and say that Laclos's novel is about *how* things mean, the process of signifying. We have seen that this question has intrigued readers of the novel as different as Madame Riccoboni, the Bishop of Pavia, Baudelaire, Gide, Malraux, and a host of twentieth-century critics. Laclos's strategy should be clear by now: through careful control of his text, he intended to disrupt the generic and stylistic expectations of the reader, make the letters resist traditional interpretive methods, while luring the reader into the trap of insisting on a stable, final significance. The point(s) of exasperation, mirrored in Valmont's tardy discovery in Letter 142 that "I don't know whether I misread or misunderstood your letter" (p. 336), should become the point(s) of comprehension, leading the reader to question his own "meaning-making" processes. Working against the backdrop of the Enlightenment, and such intellectual endeavors as the *Encyclopédie,* Laclos was not unaware of the exhilaration and danger inherent in any systematic inquiry. The *liaisons dangereuses* are those cultural structures in which we place too much confidence, and their "danger" increases when any part of the critical consciousness begins to atrophy. Even the "best" minds are lured by promises of control through knowledge, be they minds like Valmont and Merteuil, or minds like those of us who ponder the "meaning" of *Les Liaisons dangereuses.*

CHAPTER 5

One Dangerous Connection

I *Introduction*

SOMETIME in the 1850s, Baudelaire sketched out a projected essay on *Les Liaisons dangereuses*. First published in 1903, these haphazard notes give a rare view of what the nineteenth century's greatest poet thought was significant in Laclos's novel. Under the rubric "Intrigue," or "Plot," Baudelaire's first notation reads: "Comment vint la brouille entre Valmont et la Merteuil. Pourquoi elle devait venir" ("How the falling-out between Valmont and Merteuil came about. Why it had to happen").[1] He saw clearly that, despite the importance of the other relationships in the novel, it was essential to understand this one if the others were to be analyzed adequately. Other of the novel's more perspicacious critics have since intuited that the pyrotechnics of this pair's actions toward their victims should not detract from their own interaction.[2] Henri Duranton, in his perceptive article,[3] suggests that the most satisfactory explanation of the novel rests within the Merteuil-Valmont correspondence. He concludes his study with the affirmation that their relationship is not based on equality, but rather on the need for an echo, a mirror to reflect their self-judgments. "Their complicity is illusory whether they know it or not," and their letters become a means, the only one left them, to dominate each other (pp. 139, 140). For reasons that will become clearer later in this chapter, I find Duranton's interpretation of the *Liaisons* a felicitous one. Approaching the Merteuil-Valmont "connection" from a somewhat different perspective, this chapter seeks to give the reader of *Les Liaisons dangereuses* a strategy for reading at least that part of the novel.

For instance, one of the most nettlesome questions confronting critics of *Les Liaisons dangereuses* concerns Merteuil's puzzling

114

willingness to write and send incriminating letters to Valmont — letters which finally undo her plots and her career. There is no doubt she understands that the letters are potentially harmful, as does Valmont, who reiterates for the last time at the end of the correspondence: "...[Since] each of us is in possession of all that is necessary to ruin the other, ... we have an equal interest in behaving with mutual caution" (CLIII, 357). And, throughout the novel, had she and Valmont not used those letters of their other correspondents to deceive and betray them? In her famous Letter 81, Merteuil explains in detail how she had taught herself to conceal from everyone any opinion or feeling that she did not want noticed. Why then, readers of the novel have continually asked, this contradictory behavior of writing down everything for Valmont? Was Laclos himself aware of this inconsistency? Did this apparent lack of verisimilitude escape his attention, or did he just ignore it, since Merteuil had to write the letters if the novel were to exist at all? Is there any satisfactory explanation for this apparent contradiction? Readers will not be surprised to learn that I think there is, and that, in terms of the critical model that this chapter will elucidate, Merteuil's exchange of letters with Valmont, along with other "inconsistencies" in the novel, is fully explicable. The Merteuil-Valmont correspondence is a sign of a mutual confidence that both characters wish to express: "don't hurt me; I'm not going to hurt you." It is a "myth of mutual trust" which eventually degenerates to "don't hurt me *or* I will hurt you," and, finally, to "I'm going to hurt you because (I believe) you hurt me." This "myth" is, to anticipate some of the following discussion, a stabilizing mechanism which helps the Merteuil-Valmont dyad sustain at least a temporary and illusory equilibrium. This assumption of trust makes the exchange of letters possible; however, as we shall see, it is a false assumption. The ritualistic aspect of the exchange becomes perverted because the Merteuil-Valmont relationship is morbid, and finally must disintegrate.

Laclos has written a work about interpersonal relationships, and specifically about the processes of communication, emphasizing his subject by casting it in the epistolary format. An analysis of the Merteuil-Valmont correspondence is one means for examining *what* is happening in *Les Liaisons dangereuses,* a step that must be taken before the question of *why* can be answered, or even intelligently asked. Since Laclos's novel is about the processes of interpersonal communication, this chapter will use as a critical model recent work in the field of human communication and interactional psychotherapy. The analysis of certain aspects of the Merteuil-Valmont correspondence will be based on a simple premise, namely, that this particular communicational dyad is pathological. From the beginning of the novel, Laclos gives us clues, which the application of communication theory helps to decipher, that we are in the presence of a "dangerous" situation, of a communicational system which cannot avoid disintegrating. The novel's denouement, often criticized,[4] is systematically logical. This pathological relationship defines all the other relationships in the novel (including that between the novel's letter writers and its readers). Merteuil and Valmont do not exist apart from each other, nor should they be studied in individual isolation. They form a *system* that is created and destroyed within the limits of Laclos's fiction.

This essay, then, will have two parts. The first is an introduction for the uninitiated reader to a communicational model which produces felicitous results when applied to epistolary fiction. The second part will be an analysis, in terms of this model, of *Les Liaisons dangereuses,* and especially of the Merteuil-Valmont relationship. A study will be made of the communicational sequences which compose the whole system as we receive it from the novel.[5]

II   *The Model*

Most agree that *Les Liaisons dangereuses* is a novel about, among other things, the dynamics of human communication. Todorov's brilliant interpretation of the novel, using as his model the "speech-act" theories of J. L. Austin and J. R. Searle, has made us aware of this aspect.[6] Nonetheless, a more appropriate model for such an analysis may be found in the writings of a group of men and women, led by Dr. Paul Watzlawick, variously called "the Palo Alto Group," "communicational therapists," and "interactional or family psychotherapists," who, over the past fifteen years or so, have been making "the first concerted attempt to apply systems-theory concepts to the practice of psychotherapy."[7] The group (one hesitates to write "school," though the success and influence of the "group" may soon weaken that hesitation) has as its mentor Gregory Bateson, the biologist and anthropologist, whose work in many fields, most significantly perhaps with the concept of schizophrenia, served as a starting point for their most consistent theories.[8]

For present purposes, I will present only the essential principles which support and explain the work of these theories. First, as they state in a recent publication, these therapists study "process rather than content, and the here and now rather than the past."[9] Second, they believe that much psychological disorder is caused by communicational disorders in the sequences of interaction between two or more communicants who form a system or "family." More specifically, the inability to *metacommunicate,* that is, to communicate about communication, is the most frequent case of psychopathologies.[10] Third, it is held that information and systems theory (more generally, cybernetics) has much to offer in terms of models by which the initiated can interpret a "dysfunctional relationship." Fourth, the focus of study and analysis is not the individual but rather the *circuit,* the reception and use of the message. Fifth, every message has two kinds of meaning, that of report and command, and it is impossible to separate these two meanings without affecting the interpretation of the whole system. No communicational event is, or can be, isolated from the whole process of which it is part. No one event (for example, letter or part of a letter) can be said to be the "cause" of what follows, and no single event can be seen as an isolated "effect"; every effect is a cause, and vice versa.

Last, this group of scientists believes that at the base of man's communicational problems there is a system of paradoxes, and that when man learns to handle them, he will be able to communicate with a minimum of misunderstanding. The best-known of these paradoxes is explained in Bateson's "double-bind" theory. Briefly, a "double-bind" situation occurs when two or more persons are involved in an intense relationship of repeated experiences. Messages are given that assert something but that also simultaneously comment on that assertion; these two assertions are mutually exclusive. A simple and nonthreatening example is a sign on the wall that states: DO NOT READ THIS SIGN! The injunction must be disobeyed to be obeyed, thereby causing some anxiety. If two people are involved, such a situation can lead to the disconfirmation of one's concept of self and often to schizophrenia. For those not conditioned to perceive their world in double-bind patterns, such situations can be intolerable, especially for children in a pathological familial relationship.

The specifics of these principles will be examined when we analyze the Merteuil-Valmont relationship. However, I would like first to acquaint the reader with the way that this group organizes these principles in their most influential work, *The Pragmatics of Human Communication: A Study of Interactional Patterns, Pathologies, and Paradoxes.*[11] This study "deals with the pragmatic (behavioral) effects of human communication, with special attention to behavioral disorders" (p. 13). The attention of these investigators is focused, almost solely, on the *relationship* and its significance to the larger *system.* To aid them in the application of their theories, they have offered five "tentative axioms of communication" to which I will refer in my analysis of *Les Liaisons dangereuses.* The corollaries of these axioms are their pathological responses; when any or all of these axioms are ignored or "disturbed," the communicational process itself becomes "dysfunctional," that is, it fails to serve its intended purpose.

The first axiom posits that it is impossible *not* to communicate. Silence, ignoring messages or signals, absence: all these forms of behavior are means of communicating. Once someone initiates a communicational exchange, it is impossible *not* to respond. This axiom forms one of the bases of the group's theory of schizophrenia: "It appears that the schizophrenic tries *not to communicate.* But since even nonsense, silence, withdrawal, immobility (postural silence), or any form of denial is itself a communication, the schizophrenic is faced with the impossible task of denying that he is communicating and at the same time denying that his denial is a communication" (pp. 50–51). On some levels, Madame de Tourvel's attitudes in Laclos's novel, as she tries to avoid communicating with Valmont, can be considered homologous to a state that would be defined today as schizophrenic.

The second axiom holds that every communication has two levels of meaning: it "not only conveys information [the content level], but ... at the same time it imposes behavior [the relationship level]" (p. 51). Depending on the success ("healthiness") or lack of success ("sickness") of the communicational sequence, the content level or the relationship level is dominant. "The ability to metacommunicate appropriately [that is, to communicate on the relationship level] is not only the *conditio sine qua non* of successful communication, but is intimately linked with the enormous problem of awareness of self and others" (p. 53). This axiom is especially significant in any discussion of the Merteuil-Valmont interaction. Their inability to leave the frame of content and examine the frame of relationship is the most direct cause of the disintegration of their "connection." To summarize: "Every communication has a content and a relationship aspect such that the latter classifies the former and is therefore a *metacommunication*" (p. 54).

The third axiom states that "the nature of a relationship is contingent upon the *punctuation* of the communicational sequences between the communicants" (p. 59). "Punctuation" refers to the attempts of the participants in an interaction to organize a communicational sequence "so that it will appear that [one or the other] has initiative, dominance, dependency or the like" (p. 56) in terms of the other members of the system. A roughly synonymous term for "mispunctuation" would be "misinterpretation." A common example in family therapy is when a husband blames his inactivity on his wife's nagging, while she explains her nagging as a means of getting him to act. Again, their inability to metacommunicate often results in an interminable, oscillating series of exchanges. The question facing the therapist is not who is right or wrong, but *how* to make the participants see that they are not correctly "punctuating" their interactions. In another type of interaction, the common result of such "mispunctuation" could be war. An example: Country *A* begins stockpiling nuclear devices because Country *B* has "threatened" the former by so doing. But Country *B* says it was only "defending" itself by trying to gain parity with Country *A*. Each party is "mispunctuating" — really "misinterpreting" — the messages it receives from the other. Charges of "madness' or "badness" are laid at the door of one party by another because of "unresolved discrepancies in the punctuation of communicational sequences" (p. 93).

These "discrepancies" can occur in at least three different circumstances: (1) when at least one communicant does not possess the same amount of information as the other (for example, a lost letter), *but does not know this;* (2) since each person must order the immense amount of information he or she receives — a process which depends on his or her vision of "reality," a vision which often fails to coincide with that of other communicants — the potential for "mispunctuation" is manifest;[12] and, (3) when cause and effect are confused (*A* says: "I act because you act. *B* replies: "But, *I* act because *you* act," and so on). In *Les Liaisons dangereuses,* the frequency of mispunctuation accelerates as the Merteuil-Valmont relationship disintegrates.

The fourth communicational axiom of the interactional therapists is a bit complex: "Human beings communicate both digitally and analogically. Digital language has a highly complex and powerful logical syntax but lacks adequate semantics in the field of relationship, while analogic language possesses the semantics but has no adequate syntax for the unambiguous definition of the nature of relationships'' (pp. 66–67). Again to simplify, we may say that analogic communication is essentially all *nonverbal* communication, while digital communication is the more abstract, *verbal* transmission of messages. Analogic communication is made up of the clues which the context of an interaction provides (posture, movement, oral rhythm, appropriateness of event, and so forth). It is important to remember that analogic communication occurs when ''digitalization'' is not yet, or no longer, possible. ''Man is the only organism known to use both the analogic and the digital modes of communication'' (pp. 62–63). The problems that occur when either mode is misused can seriously impair a communicational sequence. ''Not only can there be no translation from the digital into the analogic mode without great loss of information, but the opposite is also extraordinarily difficult: to *talk about* relationship requires adequate translation from the analogic into the digital mode of communication'' (p. 66). Such traditional concepts as trust, sincerity, confidence can all be communicated either digitally (''I trust you won't betray me'') or analogically (for example, in the ritualistic exchange of letters between Merteuil and Valmont). However, ''there is an inevitable and significant ambiguity which both sender and receiver face,'' and it is the inadequate ''translation from one mode to another'' which causes most systems to malfunction (p. 71).

The last axiom states that ''all communicational interchanges are either *symmetrical* or *complementary,* depending on whether they are based on equality or difference'' (p. 70). Watzlawick and his group are careful to insist that no value judgments, such as ''goodness'' or ''badness,'' should be made about these two types of interaction. Most healthy relationships have elements of both types in them. However, their extremes are quite pathological and ultimately destructive. A symmetrical relationship, where one's behavior patterns and responses mirror those of another communicant (''anything you can do, I can do better''), can easily accelerate, escalate, and lead to schism. A complementary relationship, where one communicant's behavior complements another's (either in the ''one-up'' position, or the ''one-down'' position), can degenerate into the classic sadomasochistic syndrome.

One partner cannot independently impose one type of relationship on the other; *both* must "agree" that the relationship is going to be either symmetrical or complementary or both. Again, it is a question of equilibrium in these relationships, not of whether they are inherently good or bad as communicational postures. A healthy relationship is "a flexible alternation of symmetrical with complementary interchanges" (p. 115). The exchange between Valmont and Merteuil vacillates wildly between "symmetricality" and "complementarity," never attaining a final equilibrium. The result is that their essentially symmetrical relationship escalates into "war." Most, if not all, of the relationships between these two protagonists and the rest of the novel's personages — especially the one between Valmont and Tourvel — are complementary ones. Obviously, then, the novel's tension, and final success, results from the instability of the Merteuil-Valmont relationship.

Watzlawick's group is aware that their axioms are tentative, "rather informally defined and certainly more preliminary than exhaustive" (p. 70). Yet they can help the critic to speak in more rigorous terms about epistolary fiction (and, for that matter, about many types of fiction, especially drama[13]). The significance of this model is that it emphasizes the multifaceted *relationships* with which any sociocentric literature must deal. When using it, the critic has the freedom to concentrate on actions, to describe them, and to lead the reader to understand that meaning (even language itself) is not immanently defined but is understandable only in terms of how it regulates, and is itself regulated, by interpersonal behavior or interactional events.

These principles form a useful critical model that can enable us to comprehend the complexity of *Les Liaisons dangereuses*. Despite several recent efforts, there has been no satisfactory analysis of how a writer sets up a system of communicational interchanges in a work of fiction, presents the functioning of the system, and finally the success, or more often than not, the lack of success of that system. The present essay will undertake such an analysis.

III   *The Connection*

Again, there are few readers who would disagree that one of the subjects of *Les Liaisons dangereuses* concerns the uses and misuses of information, or that the novel is almost exclusively about how people communicate. Every relationship, every desire, every other thought or idea in the novel goes back to the central principle on which it is based: all behavior eventually becomes communicational. Laclos's choice of the epistolary format was not a coincidence. Besides the traditional artistic reasons which may have made him more susceptible to using this format rather than another, there is the obvious reason that he saw an opportunity to sum up what the novel as a genre was about, and to point it in the direction it should go. Also, he must have seen a tantalizing chance to comment on the very nature of the cultural codes of the Enlightenment, and especially on the limitations of an ideology predicated on the organization and diffusion of information.

In absolute terms, the purposes of information are distorted if they are misused, misappropriated, and misunderstood, or mistransmitted. Patterns of communicational interchanges must be discovered and understood if information is to be beneficial. "Dangerous connections" are those interstices in an information system that malfunction, throw the system out of equilibrium, and ultimately cause the system to disintegrate. These "connections" cannot be separated from the system, isolated and repaired; the *whole system* has to be rehabilitated, either through some sort of stabilizing process from within (and, in many cases, this is only a temporary process and not one which restructures) or through some sort of intervention from without the system. Laclos wrote a novel that could end in no other way than it did. It is a carefully plotted narrative about the dysfunction of a communicational system, dysfunctional because it was insufficient to meet the demands of its users.

The success of the Merteuil-Valmont relationship is in question from the initial words of Merteuil's first letter to Valmont:

Come back, my dear Vicomte, come back: what are you doing? . . . Leave at once: I need you. I have had an excellent idea and I want to put its execution in your hands. These few words should be enough; only too honoured by this mark of my consideration, you should come, eagerly, and take my orders on your knees. . . . You will receive this letter tomorrow morning. I insist on your being at my house at seven o'clock in the evening. . . . At eight I shall give you your liberty. (II, 25–26)

Throughout this letter, Merteuil cajoles, threatens, and entices Valmont to return to Paris. The tone and vocabulary are somewhat traditional: pouting, mock threats, reminders that she is attractive, and so forth. Alone, or even with a few of Valmont's responses, this initial letter could provide little information about the pathological nature of the relationship. However, this "playful" tone will become a dominant and nasty one and, through the process of symmetrical escalation, will explode into "war." Valmont's response hints at these developments: "Your orders are charming; your manner of giving them still more delightful; you would make tyranny itself adored" (IV, 28). But he "must" disobey her, because he too has a project which is worthy of both of them. "Don't be angry; listen. I am going to tell you, the confidante of all my inmost secrets, the most ambitious plan I have yet conceived" (IV, 28). In this way, the tone of the relationship is established; there is still time to change it, but neither communicant will be willing or able to metacommunicate sufficiently to do so. There follows a correspondence of fifty-three letters (twenty-one from Merteuil; thirty-two from Valmont; there are one hundred and seventy-five letters in the whole collection) which shows a series of abortive attempts by each to establish superiority over the other, to change the direction of the relationship, to define the nature of the exchange. All these attempts will, however, be within the framework of their interaction, and, as Bateson has shown, only paradox can result when efforts to define a relationship are made in terms of that relationship.[14]

In the exchange outlined above, Merteuil and Valmont are both trying to establish primacy in determining who controls their relationship. It is still on the level of social generalities and love formulas, however. Only in rereading these passages, after having read the entire novel in terms of the communication theory outlined here, do these seemingly innocent series of parries and thrusts become more sinister.

Letter 4 is also significant because Valmont mentions the two stabilizing mechanisms that will be used by both correspondents to maintain their system and as relationship rules to govern it. Without these rules, as we will see at the end of the novel, the system self-destructs. These mechanisms, which act as forms of negative feedback to neutralize possible dysfunctions, are the "myth of sexual compatibility" and the "myth of mutual trust." (We have looked at the latter in the introduction to this essay; however, I would like to draw the reader's attention to the significance, for the "myth of mutual trust," of Valmont's incredible claim that Merteuil is the "confidante of all my inmost secrets." This remark will return to haunt him later.) As for the other "myth," there are numerous references throughout the novel, by both Merteuil and

Valmont, to the fact that their sexual relationship, sometime in the past, was a perfect one. Both of them realized that there could be no ulterior motives in their liaison since the sexual game plan of one was neutralized by the acumen and knowledge of the other. There was no fear of gossip, of loss of reputation, because each "respected" the other. Now, however, both use this myth of mutual compatibility (on the sexual level) to remind each other of what awaits after their projects are completed: "Perhaps at the end of the course we shall meet again," says Valmont (IV, 28). Merteuil, in a momentarily nostalgic aside late in the correspondence, reflects back upon that happy, satisfying time when they were "in love": "Do you know that I sometimes regret that we are reduced to such courses. There was a time when we loved each other — for it was, I think, love — and I was happy; and you, Vicomte! ... But why think now of a happiness which can never return?" (CXXXI, 314). The myth of sexual compatibility, that there were no "games" between them on that level, finally had to be discarded. It had acted as instigator of the correspondence ("here's a chance for us to get together again") and as a guarantee of good faith ("succeed and we can take up where we left off"), but it was a "myth," destroyable and unrecoverable.

It will be remembered that all sequences of communicational interaction can be described in terms of symmetrical or complementary relationships, that is, as "relationships based on either equality or difference" (p. 68). The relationship we are analyzing here is primarily a symmetrical one, though there are occasional brief sequences where one or the other communicant attempts to establish a complementary pattern (see, for example, Letters 129 and 131). Such relationships can be seen as a game of "one-upmanship." The purpose of the game is to see who controls the exchange. As the game progresses, the "anything-you-can-do-I-can-do-better" syndrome accelerates until there is no other way to prove superiority than to attack each other (see Letter 153 from Valmont to Merteuil, and the latter's brief response: "Very well: war."). The connection short-circuits. Both participants, unable to comment on or, in fact, perceive the framework of their relationship because they are unable to move to a higher order of knowledge and thus of communication, end by destroying each other. We have already seen how Letters 2 and 4 began this series of "one-upmanship" responses. The entire exchange or sequence which begins the *Liaisons* (Letters 2, 4, 5, 6, 10, 15, and 20, with Letters 2,

5, 10, and 20 written by Merteuil) leaves no doubt about the direction of the couple's relationship. Valmont refuses, in Letter 4, to take up Merteuil's challenge, at least for now. Merteuil's answer, again in a tone of restrained and coy anger, is an attempt to retain the upper hand: "Do you know, Vicomte, that your letter is most extraordinarily insolent and that I might very well be angry? It proves clearly, however, that you are out of your mind; and that, if nothing else, spares you my indignation" (V, 30). She begins what will be a series of mocking passages and letters about Valmont's plans to "have" the Présidente, one of their society's most famous prudes — and married at that! How ridiculous to cuckold a husband! "[If] you refuse to obey me. . ., I am tempted at this moment to believe you do not deserve your reputation. What is more, I am tempted to withdraw the confidence I have placed in you" (IV, 31). In other words, "perhaps I can't trust you anymore; perhaps we should end our epistolary connection."

Valmont's response will become typical of him. He tries, in Letter 6, to place Merteuil with all other women who use their intimate relationship with men to distract them from their projects. He reminds her that their "friendship" might not sustain further remarks about Tourvel's character from Merteuil, thereby giving her a handle on his ego. He then explains why Tourvel is exceptional: she is an anticoquette. Then, in a brief attempt to comment on his own interaction with Merteuil, Valmont makes a metacommunicational statement: "Soyons de bonne foi." "Let's be frank" and remember that our friendship is unique, outside the order of relationships like the one I want with Tourvel. However, in order to keep Merteuil's respect, he tells her (and will tell her countless times) of how "hypocritical" he is with Tourvel: "As you see, I am not lost beyond recall" (VI, 34). In her response three days later (Letter 10), Merteuil uses a device especially suited to epistolary discourse: she throws Valmont's own words, taken out of context, back at him. She insists on having the last word. And, for the first time, she accuses him of breaking another of the rules of their relationship: "you might as well be in love," which will become a few lines further on "you are in love" (X, 39, 40). This will be a charge against which Valmont will argue until the final exchange of the correspondence. It is an important leitmotif because it implies that one member of the couple is not playing by the mutually accepted rules of the game. Merteuil treats Valmont as a wayward pupil in this letter, rejecting his desired autonomy, and suggesting, as she tries to punctuate their relationship, that he is not well: "But you — you are no longer yourself: you behave as if you were afraid of succeeding.... Write to me, at least, more often than you do and keep me informed of your progress" (X, 40). Hers is a constant effort to place Valmont in a "one-down" situation, that is, to proffer her love and friendship on one hand, while mocking his efforts at autonomy on the other. (This is also exemplary of the classic "double-bind" theory of paradox.) In the remainder of this letter, she gives a minute account of how she manipulates Belleroche, her current lover. This passage presages the famous ones about Prévan, which we will look at below. They are reminders to Valmont which say: "Watch out; I am not a normal woman; don't treat me like one."

The last two letters of this sequence (15 and 20) retain the coy and teasing tone of the first two, but they make final one important rule of this particular phase of the couple's game, one which will be the ostensible "cause" of the relationship's destruction. Valmont, enticed by the chance to resume the sexual liaison with Merteuil, attempts a reconciliation. "And what is this of a final parting? I renounce the vows we made in that moment of delirium" (XV, 48). He implies that he might be jealous should Merteuil retain only a single lover. "Take me back, or at least take a second lover. Do not betray for the sake of a single whim the inviolable friendship to which we are sworn" (XV, 48). He admits that he is perhaps "in love" with Tourvel, but also wants to remind Merteuil that she will always be special to him. Merteuil's response is a master put-down, and, briefly, at the end of this exchange, she has succeeded in controlling their relationship. She offers a "contract" to Valmont as an answer to his "folle idée" that they resume their sexual connection:

As soon as you have seduced your Fair Devotee, as soon as you can furnish me with proof that you have done so, come to me and I shall be yours. Remember, however, that in important affairs of this kind, proof, to be valid, must be in writing. If we keep to this arrangement, I shall, on the one hand, be your reward and not your consolation, and I prefer it that way; on the other, you will add spice to your success by making it a step towards your infidelity. (XX, 55)

And so, the game becomes more complex. In order to win Merteuil again, Valmont must, from the start, renounce any autonomy regarding the interpretation of his relationship with Tourvel. By making *herself* the game's prize, Merteuil brilliantly and effectively determines how this particular game will work out. She has trapped Valmont; however, realizing that he might resent this trap, she tries to attenuate her victory by suggesting that "seriously [that is, my *real* reason, which is not to control you], I am very curious to know what a prudish woman will find to write in such circumstances..." (XX, 55). But both she and Valmont realize how important this game of one-upmanship has become, as she carefully points out earlier in this letter: "once one becomes interested in the game, there is no knowing where one will stop" (XX, 55). The seriousness of the game is emphasized, I think, by the fact that Valmont does not make specific reference to this contract until Letter 115, written two months later. But, by then, Merteuil has changed her mind, as we shall see.

So, by the end of this first series of exchanges, the two correspondents have established the parameters of the system in which they will operate. These parameters are discovered through a process of trial and error, of feints and retreats, not unlike the maneuvers of skirmishers who precede two large armies seeking out each other's weaknesses and strengths. Each knows how far to go, and the stabilizing mechanisms of the system are established and readied for use. In this particular "subgame" of the larger game, Merteuil also introduces a prize which will serve to "reward" Valmont, a prize he must seek if he is to perpetuate their "myth of sexual compatibility." But the contract serves also to control him because, by accepting the prize, he will have had to accept the rules that Merteuil *herself* laid down. Likewise, the "nonprize" — what Valmont will lose if he fails to succeed — will deprive Merteuil of her own pleasure. Nothing illustrates more clearly the interdependence of these two people. They exist through and because of each other. There can be no Merteuil sans Valmont, no Valmont sans Merteuil.

IV *The Sequences*

An argument can be made that such exchanges or sequences of exchanges as the one just analyzed form a series of redundant patterns which are all similar in their run-away "symmetricality." These abortive attempts of Merteuil and Valmont at establishing complementary or static symmetrical relationships can be organized by an outside observer (Laclos, his fictional editor, us) into a finite number of sequences. I will list them below, not as a definitive division, but as a theoretical one based on my reading of how Merteuil and Valmont tentatively punctuate, or interpret, the continuous series of exchanges which make up *Les Liaisons dangereuses*. I can see at least nine such sequences, and they, of course, make up the whole system. (The division of the Merteuil-Valmont correspondence into these isolatable sequences is invalid on one level, since they have to exist as one long communicational unit or the novel cannot exist at all. My division is for illustrative purposes, then, and is not meant to substitute for the total comprehension of the system.) Each of these sequences may be analyzed *in extenso* in terms of the model that is the subject of this chapter, however, for a more effective argument, the present intention is to present the sequences with a minimum of comment, elaborating only on those events or letters that are especially illustrative of the tendencies under discussion.

Sequence I: Letters *2,* 4, *5,* 6, *10,* 15, *20*
(italicized numbers refer to letters written by Merteuil).

This sequence, the one that determines the parameters of the system as we know it, has been analyzed above.

Sequence II: Letters 21, 23, 25, *33,* 34, *38.*

This sequence is defined by an almost frenetic effort on Merteuil's part to take unquestioned control of the relationship which had been established in Sequence I. It ends when Merteuil, refusing to accept Valmont's suggestion to correspond primarily about his affair with Tourvel, imposes her own subject matter: "With nothing else to occupy me, I have amused myself with the little Volanges, and it is about her that I want to talk to you.... It is now that you could be extremely useful to me.... Finish off your Présidente, then" (XXXVIII, 89, 90). She will not allow Valmont to dictate the premises of their connection.

Sequence III: Letters 40, 44, 47, *51.*

This sequence continues efforts to direct the relationship, but here Valmont is more decisive than he was in Sequence II, writing almost solely about his affair with Tourvel. Merteuil's response is the same as in Sequence II. Increasingly, she and Valmont use the information each willingly provides the other — as demanded by the "myth of mutual trust" — to shift the focus of the relationship and to define it, each one in his own terms. As the informational aspect of the messages weakens, the pace of their system's disintegration accelerates.

Sequence IV: Letters 53, *54,* 57, 59, *63,* 66.

This sequence is almost completely controlled, again, by Merteuil. Valmont has finally become interested in her plot to seduce Cécile, and they write to each other about strategies. There is a brief moment of "complementarity" in this exchange as Merteuil strengthens her hand, reminding Valmont not to "take such a lively interest in your own affairs that you lose sight of this one; remember that it is of concern to me.... On you will depend the denouement of this intrigue" (LXIII, 137, 138). In this revealing contradiction, Merteuil asserts her supremacy, while simultaneously assuring Valmont that her success will depend on him. They need each other, but they cannot accept this fact, and refuse to recognize it. The relationship has still not resolved this fundamental inconsistency, and its failure to do so will have predictable results.

Sequence V: Letters 70, 71, *74,* 76, 79, *81, 85,* 96.

This sequence (made up almost entirely of the "Prévan episode") results in a major recalibration of the limits of the system (that is, the mechanism which equilibrates the exchange is set at a higher, and even less stable level); the danger of overloading the circuit is thereby greatly increased. Because of its significance, this sequence should be examined more closely than the others.

Merteuil's taunts about Valmont's apparent love for Tourvel lead him to respond in the first sentence of Letter 70: "I have an important warning to give you, my dear" (LXX, 148). The warning is that Prévan, a young rake with a reputation almost as notorious as Valmont's for conquering unwilling women, has accepted the challenge of seducing the most unattainable prude of all, Madame de Merteuil. Valmont explains what sort of person Prévan is, but remains assured that Merteuil will prevail. She does not respond. Two days later, Valmont writes another letter to Merteuil in which he brags about a minor sexual victory, and he ends with the admonition: "Above, all, defend yourself from Prévan" (LXXI, 150).

Merteuil's answer is one of pique and unconcealed anger that Valmont had taken the initiative to warn *her,* thereby implying that she was incapable of handling the situation: "Since when, my dear man, have you taken to being so easily frightened? Is Prévan really so very formidable? ... You are jealous of him. Well! I am going to set [myself] up as judge between you [two]" (LXXIV, 157, 158). Valmont's answers, in Letters 76 and 79, are of a different tone from that of before; Merteuil has "misread" his intent, he insists, and she should not use Prévan as a standard against which to measure him. He professes confusion: "No matter how often I read your letter I am no further towards understanding it.... What, then, can it be taken to mean?" (LXXVI, 160). Be careful, he warns, you are playing dangerously. You are a good player, but you might trip up; "you ... have triumphed a hundred times, I consider, more through good luck than good judgement" (LXXVI, 162). And, in Letter 79, he tells a lengthy story of how Prévan got his reputation (by seducing three close friends, all newly married, simultaneously) as another type of warning to Merteuil. "It is for you to decide whether you wish to contribute to his glory, to be yoked to his triumphal car.... Remember that for the role you have elected to play, intelligence is not enough" (LXXIX, 176).

Merteuil responds with Letter 81, her "spiritual autobiography," and perhaps the best-known letter of the novel, and with Letter 85, which recapitulates her humiliation of Prévan. The first is a *command:* this is the way I want you to see me, and this is the way I see myself. The second is a *reinforcement* of this self-image: this is how I succeeded (compare Valmont's Letter 71 and his cuckolding of Vressac), therefore I deserve this image. It is not important whether Merteuil's version of the past and of her development as a coquette occurred in this way. It *is* important that this is her willed self-interpretation and that she decides to tell Valmont this story at this point in the sequence. She realizes the import of what she is doing: "Since I have begun to justify myself, I may as well do it thoroughly.... I must put you to the trouble of *studying the whole of my conduct* [*l'ensemble de ma conduite*], if you wish to achieve a knowledge of [me]" (LXXXI, 187, my italics).

Merteuil thereby illustrates one of the premises of interactional therapy: one can only understand another's conduct by studying the *ensemble,* not isolated segments. Messages must be "read" carefully and in context, or there is a risk of misunderstanding motives, thereby increasing the "misreader's" own danger. Merteuil realizes that she may seem to be justifying her actions to Valmont, but she does so because only in that way can she remind him that she is *not* a normal woman. "Now you may set your mind to rest; now, above all, you may do me justice. Listen, and never again put me on a par with other women" (LXXXV, 195). Valmont's response, in Letter 96, is long in coming, and it is only briefly congratulatory of Merteuil's victory over Prévan. Has she been waiting for his plaudits, he asks? Has his silence annoyed her? "I have always thought that the moment one no longer has anything but praise for a woman, one may be easy about her and turn to other things" (XCVI, 219). Congratulations, all the same, he says; but listen to *my* exploits now to see if I am not just as deserving of praise as you.

So ends a key sequence in the Merteuil-Valmont relationship. After this exchange, which is an integral part of the whole correspondence, there has to be a recalibration of the upper limits that Valmont and Merteuil had imposed on their game. The possible responses left to both of them have been reduced, and the escalation of their rivalry, carried out through a regular and furious exchange of letters, will grow until the correspondence itself becomes independent and destroys them. The Prévan episode is not just an interpolated story to keep the reader's attention; it is part of another strategic sequence between two people who are jockeying for superiority in a communicational exchange. And Letter 81 is but one more move, though an important one, in this strategy.

Sequence VI: Letters 99, 100, *106,* 110, *113,* 115.

For the first time, in this sequence, the system is confronted with *positive* feedback as its very existence is threatened. Merteuil's willingness to compromise, never strong, is now moribund. The "Prévan episode" severely limited the system's capacity for self-regulation. In this sequence, Valmont, at first confident about his impending victory over Tourvel, is soon devastated by her precipitous departure. He asks for Merteuil's consolation; her response, in Letter 113, is a masterpiece of put-downs, and hopes of reconciliation recede even further. The correspondence, at this point, has come full circle as Merteuil repeats her wish/command from her first letter: "Come back, Vicomte." She is now confident that she not only controls the Volanges-Gercourt intrigue, but the Valmont-Tourvel one as well. However, this sequence ends with a sinister warning from Valmont and prepares the reader for the denouement which can be said to begin with Letter 115. "It is incredible, my love, how easily two people, the moment they are separated, cease to understand each other.... *We are no longer of the same opinion about anything*" (CXV, 276, my italics). He has correctly perceived that their "connection" is becoming more dangerous; however, he still cannot divine why or how.

Sequence VII: Letters 125, *127*, 129, *131*.

There follows a period of ten days — the lengthiest in the novel — without any exchange of letters between the two protagonists. Tourvel has finally been seduced by Valmont; he is euphoric, experiencing "the delicious sensation of glory" (CXXV, 297), as he describes, again in careful detail, the conquest. And he cockily reminds Merteuil once more of his promised prize. Her response is petulant and bitter. "You will agree that, so far removed from each other in our way of thinking, we have no hope of coming to an understanding; and I am afraid it will be a long time, a very long time, before I change my views" (CXXVII, 307). She refuses to fulfill the agreement, thereby annulling the "myth of sexual compatibility" and threatening the "myth of mutual trust." Confident of Valmont's response, and wishing to underscore her own independence, Merteuil proposes an end to their uneasy alliance. We are like the two cheaters in a card game, she says, who, on learning that both are dishonest, decide to split the stakes and go home. Let's follow their example, she concludes. "Adieu, Vicomte."

Sequence VIII: Letters 133, *134*, 138, 140, *141*, 142, 144, *145*.

The weak attempts, which defined Sequence VII, to put an orderly end to the relationship did not succeed. Valmont refuses Merteuil's offer of a mutual break, and all but ignores her last letter. For what reason? Pride, fear, nostalgia? He is unclear, but he insists that he is *not* in love with Tourvel; he just needs that type of woman from time to time. But events and past threats have limited the types of responses that the couple can now make to each other. Merteuil is adamant; if you insist on continuing this relationship, she implies, I will demand sacrifices which you might not wish to make. In this way, she starts a new game which can only end with Valmont's humiliation, and a permanent complementary position, if he agrees to participate. He insists that he is not in love, but Merteuil mocks his excuses about his relationship with Tourvel, and especially his suggestion that the way things turned out was not his fault. (Such is the typical response of a person who refuses to accept responsibility for an existing failure in communication. The speaker's "helplessness" absolves him from explaining his actions.) At this point in their exchange, Merteuil takes a radical step: she moves from the ploy of getting Valmont to admit he's wrong about himself (which usually results in pathological "symmetricality") to a stratagem whereby she attempts to disconfirm Valmont's image of self, to imply that he has no identity (resulting in a pathological "complementarity"). Such a strategy is indicative of Merteuil's far higher level of anxiety at this stage of the relationship. As a result, her aggression, rooted in insecurity, becomes even more explicit. This movement to disconfirm Valmont's self is a serious one, and places him in a dilemma. He, as a consequence of Merteuil's action, must change his own concept of self, thereby complementing and supporting Merteuil's interpretation. This in itself is not "bad" if allowance is made for variation as the relationship evolves and if both communicants are comfortable.[15] But, in this case, Merteuil is forcing Valmont to disconfirm his vision of self if he wants to continue his liaison with her. He must be her slave as he was Tourvel's tyrant.

To effect this new relationship, Merteuil tells him an apocryphal tale about a man who always used the excuse "it's not my fault" to explain his behavior. A mistress, to ridicule him, sends him a *lettre de rupture,* using the refrain "it is not my fault" (CXLI, 335–36). Through this apologue, Merteuil is in fact saying that Valmont has "disturbed" their connection by implying involuntary action. He refuses to be "honest" with her. So the "it is not my fault" letter is a ridiculing device, and a punishment. She cannot and will not allow Valmont to determine their relationship by professing unconscious behavior. She encloses a copy of this fictitious letter, while promising Valmont that in her next letter "will also be contained my ultimatum on the subject of the treaty you propose to renew" (CXLI, 336). She avoids suggesting directly that Valmont send Tourvel the "it is not my fault" letter; however, her motives and wishes are clear.

He does send the letter to Tourvel, copied in his own hand, thereby disconfirming his self-image. He recounts the effect of this action, and asks for Merteuil's end of the "bargain." Her response is devastating. She laughs at him and his gullibility, continues to accuse him of being in love, and crows about her success at ending yet another liaison that she considered "dangerous":

Ah, believe me, Vicomte, when one woman takes aim at the heart of another, she rarely fails to find the vulnerable spot, and the wound she makes is incurable. While taking my aim at this one, or rather while directing yours, I had not forgotten that she was a rival whom you had temporarily preferred to me, and that, in fact, you had considered me beneath her. If my revenge misses the mark, I agree to taking the consequences. Thus, I am quite prepared for you to try everything you can: I even invite you to do so, and promise not to be annoyed when you succeed, if you succeed. I am so easy on this score, that I will press the point no further. Let us talk of other things. (CXLV, 341)

With this letter, she has severely limited Valmont's range of replies. The result must be the destruction of the relationship and of each participant.

Sequence IX: Letters 151, *152*, 153 *(153)*, 158, *159*.

Between Letters 145 and 151, Valmont and Merteuil see each other for the only time in the novel. Making good her threat, given in Letter 127, she seduces Danceny, Cécile's naive young suitor, and makes sure that Valmont "surprises" them at their assignation. The connection, always dangerous, is now broken. Valmont, in Letter 153, recognizes this in his first sentence: "I am replying immediately to your letter [Letter 152], and I shall *try to make myself clear* to you — which is not easy once you have decided not to understand" (CLIII, 357, my italics). He gives her what he believes to be a choice ("be my friend or my enemy"), but fails to see that such a "choice" ignores the real problem: they don't know how to metacommunicate about their interaction. Valmont is neither "friend" nor "enemy," nor can he be either; he is her partner in a pathological communicational relationship. It is the connection which is insufficient, not the good will or the bad faith of either of the communicants. Valmont warns Merteuil that there will be "war" should she persist in refusing to recognize at least his equality with her. Her response is well-known, scribbled at the bottom of his letter, and returned to him as a final rejection of the relationship: "Very well: war." (CLIII, 358). The final letters between them are really empty gestures: Valmont vaunts his deception of her; she writes back "adieu," and sets into motion their mutual destruction.

These nine sequences form an oscillatory progression which illustrates Bateson's theory that "every message in transit has two sorts of 'meaning.' On the one hand the message is a statement or report about events at a previous moment, and on the other it is a command — a cause of stimulus for events at a later moment."[16] Each exchange reduces the number of possible responses within the context of the relationship under analysis. Unless the participants in the exchange have established some means of metacommunicating about the structure of their relationship, there is a real danger that the options available to them, over a period of time, are so reduced that, unavoidably, the relationship must be destroyed or restructured. The Merteuil-Valmont dyad is peculiar in that neither participant wants to take a permanent, or even temporary, "one-down" or complementary position. They both persist in punctuating or interpreting their relationship in an egocentric way, and without considering the possibility of mispunctuation, either by themselves or by their partner. In other such relationships, less destructive but equally "unhealthy" alternatives may be possible, but "war" is the only option left these two. The ultimate irony in *Les Liaisons dangereuses* is that the sense of superiority to which Valmont and Merteuil desperately adhere is only another myth, created by them, and, in the end, evanescent. Again, Bateson: "The superiority of a person within his group is determined in the first instance by skillful use of his means of communication; to receive information and to give that which others need, to possess a workable concept of events, and to act accordingly, marks the successful man [and woman]."[17] The letters of Laclos's protagonists betray them, not only to others, but to each other. They cannot communicate successfully, and, as a result, they fail to impose their wills on others. Their self-created myth of superiority, like their relationship, disintegrates. They refuse to confirm each other's roles; they cannot change, and, they cease to exist as their correspondence ceases.

This analysis, and the communicational model that sustains it, is sufficient to show the richness and complexity of Laclos's novel. Such an analysis should reveal not only a perspective on the Merteuil-Valmont relationship, but on the more general problems of information transmission in a highly developed culture as well. However, it must not be forgotten that the Merteuil-Valmont connection, no matter how central to the novel's main preoccupation, is only one connection. *Les Liaisons dangereuses* is a fictional narrative whose attractive power resides in the complex intertwining and overlapping of all the correspondences in the novel. Careful attention should be paid to the Tourvel-Valmont relationship, for instance, as well as to the connections between and among the other correspondents. Also, the changes that occur in these relationships often do so after having been initiated by letters received, written, not received, and so forth. The novel is a labyrinth of connections whose significances change internally, according to the passing of information among letter writers, and, externally, according to the way in which the novel is read and reread. This chapter has presented one reading of one connection; the others await equally close attention.

CHAPTER 6

Conclusion: Laclos, Amanuensis

I *Unanswerable Questions*

IF a close study of Laclos's career and of *Les Liaisons dangereuses* yields one certainty it is that more questions about him are unanswerable than answerable. We do not know enough about his life to make anything but educated, tantalizing guesses. And the book itself, as we have learned, is willfully ambiguous, refusing to allow the reader to ground himself more than transitorily. Like any masterpiece — a term used more often than not to imply a kind of resistance to the final recovery of meaning — *Les Liaisons dangereuses* succeeds because of its ambiguity. Baudelaire, in the notes he left for a proposed study of the novel, wrote that this was a "livre essentiellement français" ("a book essentially French").[1] But, Jean Giraudoux, in a perceptive essay on Laclos and the *Liaisons,* argues the contrary, calling the novel a unique experiment in French fiction, a frightening book for the French reader. Why? "C'est que tout, caractères et action, y va là où le Français n'aime pas qu'ils se dirigent, au déchaînement" ("Because everything, characters and action, leads in a direction that the French do not like, toward rage").[2] Such contradictory views of the novel are the rule rather than the exception. The novel has attracted the attention of France's greatest writers of fiction — Sade, Stendhal, Baudelaire, Proust, Giraudoux, Malraux, to name a few — because it sits precariously on the interpretive line, defying meaning while luring us to perform the same operations as Merteuil and company to discover meaning; it demands to be reread, the desire of every novel, only to escape our intellectual grip again.

A challenging book, it cannot be neutralized, no matter how carefully a critic tries to stand away from any definitive interpretation. In fact, such a study as the present one, whose aim is essentially to provide alternative strategies for reading the *Liaisons,* cannot avoid becoming part of Laclos's game. His fortress is ostensibly breachable, like Montalembert's *fortification perpendiculaire,* devoid of intimidating bastions, yet deceptive; once inside, the would-be victor is confronted with a labyrinth of verbal and psychological casemates that eventually result in his being absorbed by the novel rather than the other way around. Fully aware of this danger, I would like to conclude this study of Laclos and *Les Liaisons dangereuses* with a series of educated deductions and possible conclusions, some audacious, others rather obvious; perhaps in this way I can impart enough of the texture of this novel and of Laclos's career so as to entice my readers to experience the exhilaration and risk the humiliation that reading this amazing book offers. Keeping Valmont's admonition in mind — "Ce sont toujours les bons nageurs qui se noient" ("It is always the good swimmers who drown," LXXVI, 161) — let us proceed to make some dangerous conclusions.

II   *Laclos Amanuensis*

Says Giradoux in his appreciation of Laclos: "Le vrai Laclos n'est nulle part dans les *Liaisons*" ("The true Laclos is nowhere evident in the *Liaisons,*" p. 73). And Henri Duranton observes in his essay that "les *Liaisons dangereuses* sont, en pratique, un texte sans auteur" ("the *Liaisons dangereuses* is, in effect, an authorless text").[3] Both these observations touch on an aspect of Laclos that has been hinted at throughout the present study, but not fully addressed. Simply put, Laclos's career was one of mediation, of maintaining a safe distance from the assumption of authorship. The artilleryman of letters was the perfect amanuensis, a secretary, a person who wrote for and about others. Every major work written by Laclos, that is, every work that brought him some recognition during his career, was mediated by someone else. There is an absence of directness, of self-attribution in Laclos's career that seems, on close analysis, purposeful. Montalembert, Orléans, Robespierre, the Jacobins, the Committee on Public Safety, Bonaparte, even Merteuil, Valmont: all of these personages and entities made use of Laclos's talents, directly and indirectly, providing him cover as well.

His profession, as a military officer and as a writer, is a combination of amanuensis — writing for others — and manipulation.

Dard, in the title of his biography, refers to Laclos as an "acteur caché" ("a hidden actor"), and his work as well as that of Caussy are filled with suggestions and claims about Laclos's putative authorship of anonymous pamphlets that appeared during the Revolution.[4] But it is not a simple question of anonymity. The Enlightenment was a period of accomplished and justified clandestinity. For all sorts of reasons, writers protected themselves, often ingeniously, from official indignation and chastisement. Yet by the time that Laclos began writing, and certainly by 1782, when the *Liaisons* appeared, such intricate maneuvering was not nearly as necessary as it had been in the middle decades of the eighteenth century. One still had to be careful, but nothing Laclos wrote was as threatening to the government and the church as the essays and fictions of a dozen *philosophes* who had preceded him. If anonymity for political reasons was not a necessary concern, why, then, did Laclos avoid taking direct, immediate responsibility for his work? Did his role as amanuensis reveal a carefully controlled stance that he wanted to project for private reasons?

This phenomenon of Laclos as amanuensis is not contrived, and, in fact, may be a key to deciphering some of the ambiguity that so completely surrounds *Les Liaisons dangereuses*. Reference has been made throughout this study to the two prefaces that introduce Laclos's novel; the so-called "editor" is Laclos's own reflection: another, fictional amanuensis who stakes his reputation on the idiosyncratic organization of the disparate letters provided him by Rosemonde's family. He eschews any responsibility for the letters or their contents; nonetheless, he subtly implies that if there is any uniqueness to this collection, it may come from the way *he* has edited the letters. In other words, he seems to say "don't blame me if, as my publisher implies, there is adverse reaction to the scabrous nature of these epistles; however, if the book is a critical and popular success, don't forget who brought it into existence." This ambivalent stance is maintained throughout 175 letters by the means of the "editor's" apparently casual footnotes. Laclos himself tries the same manuever; only a "par M. C. ... D. L. C." on the titlepage betrays an "author." His name would become known through the literary journals that announced and reviewed his book, but the protective and elusive initials on the first page of the *Liaisons* would provide a veil to refract the desired, but feared recognition that the novel brought to him. Scandal always seemed to approach but skirt Laclos: his son's premarital birth, the near-disaster from the poem about Madame du Barry, the essay on Vauban. Scandal was a dangerous game to play, but it did bring the exhilaration of recognition with it, and *Les Liaisons dangereuses*, as well as the rest of Laclos's career, is an exquisite series of feints and thrusts intended to draw attention, but almost always indirectly.

Throughout much of his military career before the Revolution, Laclos was under the orders of the Marquis de Montalembert, whose iconoclastic views on military engineering were only scarcely tolerated by his superiors. Unable to publish his own monumental attack on the accepted policy concerning the construction of French fortifications, Montalembert could only write an anonymous answer to the eulogy for Vauban by Carnot. It was Laclos, in the most audacious move of his career, who would take up his pen to attack Vauban, *but in the name of Montalembert's theories*. He was more harshly reprimanded for his *Sur l'Eloge de Vauban* than he had been for the much more "dangerous" *Liaisons*. Later, when he left the army and joined the Duc d'Orléans's coterie, it was as a secretary, again as amanuensis. Most Laclos specialists now agree that Orléans's two most important publications, ostensibly coming immediately from his own pen — his *Instructions aux Assemblées* and his *Exposé de la conduite du duc d'Orléans* — were both composed by Laclos. These writings, whose authorship Laclos never publicly admitted, would later come close to causing his execution, yet he escaped that fate. Why? Again, some have suggested because he was Robespierre's amanuensis, providing the leader with his most powerful speeches.

Laclos was as well an editor, often writing anonymous pieces for the Jacobin *Journal des Amis de la Constitution*. Such a position was ideal for a man with ideas but who wanted only partial recognition; any problems, and the editor could simply deny authorship. And this seems to be what Laclos desired: partial recognition, a reflected glory, not direct attention. When released from prison, he wrote a memoir for the Committee on Public Safety. This self-serving document was essentially a mélange of the accepted and desired goals of the Revolutionary government, a reflection of official policy. It has even been suggested that he wrote as well for Bonaparte. Again, there is no proof, just speculation. Yet what evolves from this speculation, too persistent to be dismissed, is the portrait of a man fascinated with power, but never able to assume it, attracted by the idea of public recognition but also a very secretive man, literally writing behind the scenes, hidden from the view of an audience that knew, or suspected, that he was there.

In his study of Laclos, Georges Daniel is the only other critic I know who examines, at least partially, this side of Laclos. The premise of Daniel's essay, it will be remembered, is the mutually exclusive and yet complementary roles of secrets and gossip.[5] Was Laclos anything like his nefarious characters, Daniel asks?

Nothing we know about him permits us to presume so. On the other hand, he did possess the highly developed interior form of the *homo absconditus* [the man who hides], and a quite powerful genius for extracting from the novelistic tradition an instrument capable of converting the most original side of his character into the definitive image of a whole society, and his aspiration for a hidden life [*une existence voilée*] into a relentless process of revelation [*dévoilement*]. (p. 32)

Possessed by a simultaneous fear of showing himself and a desire for recognition, Laclos turned to fiction for a resolution of his dilemma. The result was this strange, haunting novel which, like all epistolary novels, is "a manual of oblique action, a catalogue of recessed positions [*positions en retrait*]" (Daniel, p. 38). Yet, the solution to his dilemma was not to be so easily reached. *Les Liaisons dangereuses* turned out to be, as Giraudoux has so cleverly argued, a betrayal of the secrets of the Enlightenment: "Du jour où il parut, la mauvaise réputation du siècle fut consommée" ("From the day it appeared, the bad reputation of that century was established," p. 69).

The only comparison to be made between Merteuil and Valmont and their creator is that, like Laclos, they act through others in order to achieve recognition. *Les Liaisons dangereuses* can, in this context, be seen as an intricate working-out of Laclos's own desires and fears. Merteuil and Valmont know and achieve "success" only through the manipulation of others; for reasons left unclear, they are afraid to assert themselves by challenging their society directly. Their destiny is design, not, as they think, direct action and control. Baudelaire, in his notes on the *Liaisons,* makes an unwitting slip, almost a pun, that emphasizes this point. He refers to a famous comment of Valmont: "Conquérir est notre destin" ("Conquest is our destiny," IV, 28). But Baudelaire writes: "Conquérir est notre *dessein*" ("our *design,*" p. 833, my italics). Merteuil and Valmont have no link with destiny; their projects are shabby, their machinations disproportionate to their aims. All their scheming, as Baudelaire observes, is only "la stratégie pour gagner un prix très frivole" ("Strategy for winning a quite frivolous prize," p. 831). They misuse talents that the propaganda of the Enlightenment had taught were to be admired and emulated. The values and demands of their society imposed behavior on these bored geniuses that would in the end destroy them. This destruction was purgative for Laclos: a sort of justification for his own hesitancies and indirect actions. Giraudoux understood the bizarre relationship between Laclos and his two inimitable characters best. Referring to Laclos's moralistic tendencies, he writes:

> His moralizing creation and inspiration does not come from a sort of optimism, or sympathy for humanity, or from any hope for its rectification, but from a jealousy, a jealousy of the wicked and of their wickedness. While some moralists denounce evil in order to isolate it, others in order to be comfortable with it, still others consider that, in order to be wicked, one needs certain abilities or particular vices unavailable to most individuals; Laclos's type of denunciation, on the contrary, holds that evil's reputation is overrated, that the difficulties of its processes are exaggerated, and that it garners too easily for its practitioners admiration and success. (pp. 69–70)

Jealousy, then, and bitter frustration tainted by ambition: this is the moral portrait of Laclos that one reading of his life and career has provided. It is a portrait that certainly does not cause him to stand out from other men and women of letters of his time. The discrepancy between the social and literary ambitions of writers like Laclos and the opportunities afforded those ambitions by the institutions of the eighteenth century has assumed the status of cliché. Yet Laclos's career as amanuensis, both actual and metaphoric, is best explained and understood in these terms. His was a delicate activity, sometimes miscalculated, as with his essay on Vauban, but overall successful, if success is to be judged in terms of his scheme. The scheme: to assuage his desire for recognition through a strategy of displaced action, hoping that, in the end, reflected admiration would become immediate and direct. Eventually, it did, but not until long after he died along in Taranto.

Les Liaisons dangereuses was a courageous book for a man like Laclos to write. It embodied his dreams and his anxieties; it also somewhat cynically questioned the presumptions of a vainglorious age, that of the Enlightenment. There is an absence of spontaneity in the *Liaisons* that has more often than not relegated it to the status of a book about the excesses of "reason" or "intellectualism." This repression of emotion, controlled so well through hundreds of pages, was a chosen style, intended to reflect a world of repression, of missed opportunities and perverted goals. As Laclos tried to explain to Madame Riccoboni, he did not use horror and perversion to titillate; horror and perversion were the subject of his book. Is *Les Liaisons dangereuses* a masterpiece, or is it, as Giraudoux suggests, only a brilliant pastiche, or, as Versini's study unwittingly implies, the result of layers of literary and moral traditions, adroitly combined in a single successful effort by a mediocre mind? This question truly situates the so-called "enigma of Laclos." If, as Georges Daniel says, "great books are those which ... no longer need readers" (p. 93), then *Les liaisons dangereuses* is not yet, nor will it ever be great. It needs readers because Laclos wrote it in such a way as to ensure his reputation as an accomplished amanuensis, or writer for others.

Notes and References

Chapter One

1. Dard, *Le Général Choderlos de Laclos, auteur des "Liaisons dangereuses": Un Acteur caché du drame révolutionnaire, 1741-1803* (Paris, 1905), and Caussy, *Laclos, 1741 -1803* (Paris, 1905). Other studies that helped in putting order to Laclos's life and works include René Pomeau's *Laclos* (Paris, 1975), especially pp. 15-56, and his article "Le Mariage de Laclos," *Revue d'histoire littéraire de France* 68 (1968), 60-72, P.-E. Levayer, "Les Ecrits politiques de Laclos," *Revue d'histoire littéraire de France* 69 (1969), 51-60, Yvan Loiseau, "Le Vrai Laclos," in his *Rivarol suivi de "Le Vrai Laclos"* (Paris-Geneva, 1961), pp. 199-237, and the exhaustive study of Laurent Versini, *Laclos et la tradition: Essai sur les sources et techniques des "Liaisons dangereuses"* (Paris, 1968), as well as his "Laclos reconsidéré d'après la correspondance complète," in *Approches des lumières: Mélanges offerts à Jean Fabre* (Paris, 1974), pp. 547-60. Finally, the study of the reputation of *Les Liaisons dangereuses* by A. and Y. Delmas, *A la recherche des "Liaisons dangereuses"* (Paris, 1964), was also beneficial.

2. It is this edition to which I shall refer throughout this study: Choderlos de Laclos, *Oeuvres complètes* [*Les Liaisons dangereuses, De l'Education des femmes, Poésies, Critique littéraire, Sur l'Eloge de Vauban, Oeuvres politiques*], texte établi et annoté par Maurice Allem, Bibliothèque de la Pléiade (Paris, 1951). The only one of these works that has been translated into English is the *Liaisons;* all other translations from the French that appear in this study are mine. Future references to this edition will appear in the text as: (Allem, page number).

3. Caussy, *Laclos,* pp. 14-15. However, Caussy suspects that Laclos was not, in fact, the author of this silly poem.

4. Pomeau, *Laclos,* p. 61. Dard and Caussy also provide lively descriptions of that painful evening.

5. On this matter, see Caussy, *Laclos,* pp. 30-31.

6. Again, Caussy's recapitulation of these events is the most succinct and informative (*Laclos,* pp. 31-35). Caussy also reproduces an evaluation of Laclos by one of his superiors made sometime after 1782. It reads: "Has a good deal of intelligence, talent and even genius; nature and chance have provided him the double advantage of succeeding at the same

time in literature and making progress in the artillery arts, such that he will complete with distinction all of the tasks seen fit to assign him" (p. 34).

7. See Pomeau's informative article, "Le Mariage de Laclos," for details on Mademoiselle Duperré's family and her courtship with Laclos.

8. The three "essays" on women written by Laclos are collected together in Allem's edition under the general rubric, "De l'Education des femmes" (pp. 403–58). These writings did not appear in print until early in this century, the first two parts in 1903, and the third in 1908 (see Allem's bibliography, p. 736, for details).

Two useful studies on these pieces are those of Madeleine Raaphorst, "Choderlos de Laclos et l'éducation des femmes au XVIIIe siècle," *Rice University Studies* 53 (1967), 33–41, and Paul Hoffman, "Aspects de la condition féminine dans *Les Liaisons dangereuses* de Choderlos de Laclos," *L'Information littéraire* 15 (1963), 47–53. Hoffman's short essay is especially rich in interpretive detail.

9. The best are Hoffman's excellent "Aspects de la condition féminine," cited above, and Nancy K. Miller's two subtle and compelling studies, "The Exquisite Cadavers: Women in Eighteenth-Century Fiction," *Diacritics* 5 (1975), 37–43, and "Female Sexuality and Narrative Structures in *La Nouvelle Héloïse* and *Les Liaisons dangereuses*," *Signs* 1 (1976), 609–38.

10. On this aspect of Marivaux's work, see my study, *Marivaux's Novels* (London and Cranbury, N.J., 1974), especially chapter 2.

11. For detailed discussions on the matter, with unedited letters from contemporaries, see Caussy, *Laclos,* pp. 82–97, and Dard, *Le Général de Laclos,* pp. 112–26. Dard's conclusion on this episode is unequivocal: "Cette aventure eut une influence décisive sur la vie de Laclos: elle le décida à quitter l'armée" (p. 126).

12. For instance, Alfred Cobban, in his *A History of Modern France,* vol. I, *Old Régime and Revolution, 1715–1799* (London, 1957; rpt. 1963), suggests that the Orleanist plot was "exaggerated" (p. 148).

13. Dard, and to a lesser extent, Caussy concentrate their efforts on Laclos's role in the Revolution. Over half of both books examine in minute detail this part of Laclos's life. On the other hand, I have consulted no major studies of that cataclysm that even mention Laclos, much less give him the major role that his two biographers do. Yvan Loiseau, in his "Le Vrai Laclos," contends that the true extent of Laclos's activities during this period will never be fully known because the Duc d'Orléans's papers were destroyed by Napoleon and Louis-Philippe, the Duc's son and the last king of France.

14. The best article on Laclos's political writings is that of Paul-Edouard Levayer, "Les Ecrits politiques de Laclos," which corrects and adds to the data furnished by Dard, Caussy, and Allem. In his article, Levayer asserts that Laclos was the author of the Duc d'Orléans's *Instructions données ... à des représentants aux bailliages,* the *Exposé de la Con-*

duite du duc d'Orléans, and of most of the Duc's public and political correspondence (pp. 51-54). Also, he gives a tentative list of the texts, amounting to fewer than a hundred pages, that Laclos most likely wrote while editor of the *Journal des Amis* in 1790-91 (pp. 54-59).

15. *Lettres inédites de Laclos* (Paris, 1904), ed. Louis de Chauvigny. References will be to this edition and will appear in the text; translations are mine. There are about ninety letters to his wife in the collection, dating from April 1794 (six months after his second incarceration) and ending with his death in Taranto. Chauvigny, not unlike the fictional editor of the *Liaisons,* tells us that he has edited and excluded some of Laclos's letters, but L. Versini has promised a new, corrected edition soon.

16. Caussy, *Laclos,* p. 284, note 1. Caussy views this entire memoir on the merits of political war as a recapitulation of governmental opinion and political gossip. In other words, though well-argued, it is an unoriginal document.

17. See, for example, Caussy, *Laclos,* pp. 294-95.

18. On this piece, see Claude Pichois, "Un Roman méconnu et inachevé de Choderlos de Laclos," *Saggi e ricerche di letteratura francese* (Milano, 1960), I, 87-148, and Graham E. Rodmell, "Laclos's Other Novel," *Nottingham French Studies* 3 (1964), 63-72. Rodmell contends, and justifiably so, that the text to which Pichois refers is at best a bowderlized adaptation of some remarks probably made by Laclos in 1802. The play to which they refer was written by Pierre-Louis Lacretelle and was called *Jeune Malherbe ou le Fils naturel.* Laclos's commentary is to be found on pp. 102-48 of Pichois's study as well as in the *Oeuvres de P.L. Lacretelle aîné* (Paris, 1824), vol. IV, part 2, pp. 3-60.

19. Laclos had written one more piece whose manuscript has come down to us. It was a critique, really an encomium to the author and to French exploration, of La Pérouse's account (1790) of his voyage to the South Pacific. This work was never published by Laclos; it may be found in Allem, pp. 522-39.

20. This letter is in Chauvigny's edition; it may also be found in Caussy, *Laclos,* note 2, pp. 326-27, in Dard, *Le Général de Laclos,* pp. 473-74, and in Loiseau, "Le Vrai Laclos," pp. 233-34.

21. Two posthumous events are worth noting. Laclos was buried on an island in the Bay of Taranto, and a statue was erected in his memory. In 1815, when the Bourbons regained the throne of Naples, his tomb was opened and his ashes thrown to the wind. As for his family, though Bonaparte awarded them a pension, it was only 1000 *livres;* however, due to some residual luck of Laclos, they benefitted financially from mining shares that became income-producing after the general's death.

Chapter Two

1. In her *Laclos and the Epistolary Novel* (Geneva, 1963), pp. 26-27.

2. In his *Laclos, 1741–1803* (Paris, 1905), p. 25.

3. In his *Le Général Choderlos de Laclos* (Paris, 1905), pp. 29–32.

4. Pomeau, *Laclos,* (Paris, 1975), pp. 22–23.

5. In his articles, "Contribution bibliographique à l'étude des éditions des *Liaisons dangereuses* portant le millésime 1782," *Bulletin du Bibliophile,* no. 2 (1958), pp. 49–173, and, no. 1 (1961), pp. 44–56. Says Brun: "We do not know another book of the eighteenth century having such a performance" (p. 152).

6. Jean-Luc Seylaz, *"Les Liaisons dangereuses" et la création romanesque chez Laclos* (Geneva, 1965), p. 38. On the other hand, Dorothy Thelander believes that "from the standpoint of plot structure, a strong argument could be advanced for the original division [70 and 105 letters]" (p. 24), though this argument is not made.

7. This and the other contemporary reactions to *Les Liaisons dangereuses* to which I will refer in this chapter may be found in the Allem edition of Laclos's *Oeuvres complètes,* pp. 698–721. References will be to this edition and will appear in the text.

8. In the second half of the eighteenth century, there were essentially two types of *permissions* to publish: the *permission publique* (or *privilège*) and the *permission tacite*. The first was the formal accord granted those books which were seen as unambiguously favorable to the public welfare; the second, however, and there were many of this kind, were, as Robert Darnton has said, "for books that censors would not openly certify as inoffensive to morals, religion, or the state.... The *permissions tacites* became a paralegal loophole through which many Enlightenment works reached the market during the last half of the century." For a rich discussion of book-publishing in France at this time, see Robert Darnton's "Reading, Writing and Publishing in Eighteenth-Century France: A Case Study in the Sociology of Literature," *Daedalus,* no. 100 (1971), pp. 214–56. One of the more byzantine aspects of the *permission tacite* is that the publisher was expected to provide a foreign imprint for such books; this is why Durand *neveu's* title page for the *Liaisons* has "à Amsterdam" as its place of publication, though there is and was no doubt that the novel was published in Paris.

9. These letters were published during Laclos's lifetime, most likely with his knowledge and permission. They first appeared in the 1787 edition of *Les Liaisons dangereuses* along with some of his poems. My references will again be to the Allem edition and page numbers will appear in the text.

10. I remind the reader that page references are to the translation of P. W. K. Stone, in the Penguin Books edition of *Les Liaisons dangereuses* (Baltimore and Harmondsworth, England, 1961; rpt. 1963, 1972). Although the letter numbers in this edition are in arabic numerals, when juxtaposed in my text with page references, I will indicate letters and page thus: XV, 93, meaning Letter 15, p. 93 of the Penguin edition.

11. This term comes from Seylaz, p. 75, as does some of the discussion that follows on the "geométry" of Laclos's narrative.

12. Seylaz, *"Les Liaisons dangereuses,"* p. 29. Seylaz also examines some of the rearrangements made by Laclos as he finished his manuscript. They are not too significant, but they do show that Laclos wanted the most precise and beneficial relationship possible between and among letters as they were read. There are seven of these shifts: originally, Letter 103 followed Letter 106, 160 followed 161, the sequence 15–24 was 15, 21, 22, 23, 20, 16, 17, 18, 19, 24; the sequence 44–49 was 44, 46, 47, 48, 45, 49; the sequence 63–68 was 63, 67, 64, 65, 66, 68; the sequence 88–92 was 90, 91, 88, 89, 92, and, finally, the sequence 144–148 was 144, 147, 146, 145, 148.

13. See, for example, Dard, *Le Général Choderlos de Laclos,* pp. 48–50; Caussy, *Laclos,* pp. 29–31; André Monglond, "Clés dauphinoises des *Liaisons dangereuses,"* *Almanach du Dauphiné* (Gap, 1937), pp. 40–44; Basil Guy, "The Prince de Ligne, Laclos and the *Liaisons dangereuses:* Two Notes," *Romanic Review* 55 (1964), 260–67; and René Pomeau, "Laclos ou Valmont," chapter 2 of his *Laclos,* pp. 15–30.

14. Brooks, *The Novel of Worldliness* (Princeton, 1969), p. 78.

15. Two of the best of these are Seylaz's study and Clifton Cherpack's modest note on the *confiance/confidence* structure in the novel: "A New Look at *Les Liaisons dangereuses,"* *MLN* 74 (1959), 513–21.

16. Madeleine B. Therrien, *"Les Liaisons dangereuses":* Une interprétation psychologique (Paris, 1973), p. 31.

17. Sylvère Lotringer, "Vice de forme," *Critique,* no. 27 (1971), p. 200.

18. On the topic of boredom, see my forthcoming study, "Boredom and Meaning: A Reading of Laclos's *Les Liaisons dangereuses,"* which examines the thematic and rhetorical uses of boredom in Laclos's novel.

19. Georges Daniel, *Fatalité du secret et fatalité du bavardage au XVIIIe siècle: La marquise de Merteuil* [*et*] *Jean-François Rameau* (Paris, 1966), pp. 13–99.

20. Ibid., p. 95.

21. Jean Giraudoux, in a perceptive article on Laclos, suggests that the not-too-successful military officer, jealous of the success of such wrongdoers as Merteuil and Valmont, of the surfeit of credit given those who succeed in evil, published his novel as a means of getting even. See his "Choderlos de Laclos," *Littérature* (Paris, 1941), pp. 65–88, and chapter 6 of this study for a development of this interpretation.

22. Miller, "Female Sexuality and Narrative Structure in *La Nouvelle Héloïse* and *Les Liaisons dangereuses,"* p. 630. Miller elaborates on the enormity of Tourvel's "fall" and on Valmont's part in it, concluding that "Valmont's project, then, involves more than the seduction of a difficult subject; it requires the transformation of that object [that is, of Tourvel, into a desiring object]," and that "Mme de Tourvel and Julie are both attracted to a concept of love purified and de-sexualized by the exercise of

virtue.... The real victory sought is to force the lover to accept voluntarily what essentially amounts to a castration in the name of love..., love, in a word, that women can control'' (pp. 633–34). This is one of the best analyses available on the character of Tourvel.

23. Implied here is Valmont's suicide, a not farfetched interpretation of his death at the hands of Danceny. For one critic's view, see Daniel, *Fatalité du secret,* pp. 87–90.

24. Pichois, "Un Roman méconnu de Laclos," p. 130. Subsequent references to this text will appear in the text.

25. Lotringer, "Vice de forme," p. 201.

26. This interpretation, or variations on it, is so widespread as to make references to it unwarranted. However, Roger Vailland's *Laclos par lui-même* (Paris, 1953) is an intelligent, Marxist adaptation of this reading, and would make of Tourvel the first great bourgeoise heroine (see especially pp. 33–54).

27. Malraux, "Laclos et *Les Liaisons dangereuses,*" in his *Le Triangle noir: Laclos, Goya, Saint-Just* (1939; rpt. Paris, 1970), p. 31.

28. Duranton, "*Les Liaisons dangereuses* ou le miroir ennemi," *Revue des sciences humaines* no. 153 (1974), pp. 125–43. Future page references will be found in the text.

29. Ibid.; see especially pp. 134–37, where he emphasizes the libertine's belief that man is the sum of his senses, that *all* obstacles to the satisfaction of sensual appetites must be overcome, that the master-slave structure defines all relationships, that the libertine must never succumb to love, that he must protect himself with intricate guarantees against exposure, that he has to control public opinion, and that he should avoid at all costs a fate literally worse than death: ridicule.

30. Brooks, *The Novel of Worldliness,* Daniel, *Fatalité du secret et fatalité du bavardage,* and Malraux, "Laclos."

Chapter Three

1. There are only a few studies of the formal and generic possibilities of epistolary fiction. Among the best are François Jost, "Le Roman épistolaire et la technique narrative au XVIIIe siècle," *Comparative Literature Studies* 3 (1966), 397–427, and "L'Evolution d'un genre: le roman épistolaire dans les lettres occidentales," in his *Essais de littérature comparée,* vol. 2 (*Europaena*), pp. 89–179, 380–402; Jean Rousset, "Le Roman par lettres," in his *Forme et signification. Essais sur les structures littéraires de Corneille à Claudel* (Paris, 1964), pp. 65–108, and "La Monodie épistolaire: Crébillon fils" in his *Narcisse romancier: Essai sur la première personne dans le roman* (Paris, 1973), pp. 114–26. See also Jean-Luc Seylaz, *Les "Liaisons dangereuses" et la création romanesque chez Laclos* (Geneva, 1958), Pierre Testud, "*Les Lettres persanes,* roman épistolaire,"

Revue d'histoire littéraire de France 66 (1966), 642–56, and, T. Todorov, *Littérature et signification* (Paris, 1967). Finally, there is an excellent Ph.D. dissertation by Janet Altman, entitled "Epistolarity: Approaches to a Form" (Yale University, 1973).

2. Montesquieu, *Lettres persanes,* ed. P. Cernière (Paris, 1961), p. 332. Subsequent references will be to this edition and will appear in the text.

3. Guilleragues, *Lettres portugaises,* ed. F. Deloffre (Paris, 1962), p. 39. Subsequent references will be to this edition and will appear in the text.

4. Rousseau, *Julie, ou La Nouvelle Héloïse,* ed. Pomeau (Paris, 1960), p. 5. Subsequent references to this edition will appear in the text.

5. Graffigny, *Lettres d'une Péruvienne* (Paris, n.d.), Letter 4, p. 49. Subsequent references to this edition will appear in the text.

6. Rousset, *Forme et signification,* p. 78.

7. Altman, "Epistolarity: Approaches to a Form," p. 243.

8. The most helpful studies on time are those of Altman, especially chapter 4, A. A. Mendilow, *Time and the Novel* (New York, 1952), Georges Poulet, *Studies in Human Time* (Baltimore, 1956) and *The Interior Distance* (Baltimore, 1959), and especially Gérard Genette, *Figures III* (Paris, 1972). Also useful was Todorov's "Catégories du récit littéraire," *Communications* 8 (1966), 125–51.

9. Metz, *Essais sur la signification au cinéma* (Paris, 1968), p. 27.

10. See René Wellek and Austin Warren, *Theory of Literature* (New York, 1942; 3d edition, 1956), pp. 218–19. Also, on this very complex question, see Genette's *Figures III,* cited above, especially pp. 77 and following.

11. *History of Sir Charles Grandison,* ed. William L. Phelps, I, xxxix, vol. 13 of *The Novels of Samuel Richardson* (New York, 1901).

12. *Selected Letters of Samuel Richardson,* ed. John Carrol (Oxford, 1964), p. 63.

13. Alan D. McKillop, "Samuel Richardson: *Pamela,*" in *Twentieth-Century Interpretations of "Pamela,"* ed. R. Cowler (Englewood Cliffs, N.J., 1969), p. 27.

14. Poulet, *The Interior Distance,* pp. 56–64.

15. See especially "Catégories du récit littéraire," as well as "Choderlos de Laclos et la théorie du récit," *Tel Quel,* no. 27 (1966), 17–28, and *Littérature et signification* (Paris, 1967).

16. Altman, "Epistolarity: Approaches to a Form," p. 171.

17. Mendilow, *Time and the Novel,* p. 57.

18. Those which were particularly helpful are "Language and Human Experience," *Diogenes,* no. 51 (1965), 1–12, and the following, all of which may be found reprinted in Benveniste's *Problems in General Linguistics* (Coral Gables, Fla., 1971): "Subjectivity in Language," pp. 223–30, "Annual Communication and Human Language," pp. 49–54,

Notes and References 151

"The Nature of Pronouns," pp. 217-22, "The Correlations of Tense in the French Verb," pp. 205-15. Subsequent references to these articles will be to this translation of *Problèmes de linguistique générale,* and will appear in the text.

19. Barthes, *S/Z* (Paris, 1970), pp. 95-96. He argues as follows: "Le Récit: monnaie d'échange, objet de contrat, enjeu économique, en un mot marchandise.... Voilà la question que pose peut-être tout récit. *Contre quoi échanger le récit? Que 'vaut' le récit?...* On raconte pour obtenir en échangeant" (pp. 95, 96).

20. Duchêne, *Réalité vécue et art épistolaire: Madame de Sévigné et la lettre d'amour* (Paris, 1970). Subsequent references to this study will be found in the text.

21. In his excellent study of Diderot's novel, "The Rhetoric of *La Religieuse* and Eighteenth-Century Forensic Rhetoric," *Diderot Studies* 3 (1961), 129-54, Robert Ellrich's thesis is that, "of all Diderot's novels, *La Religieuse* is the one that most unequivocally aims to demonstrate and to persuade" (p. 130).

22. Carrol, ed., *Selected Letters of Samuel Richardson,* pp. 64, 65.

23. Cited by Carrol, p. 34. The original quote may be found in *Works of Samuel Johnson* (Oxford, 1825), VIII, 314.

24. Funt, "The Question of the Subject: Lacan and Psychoanalysis," *The Psychological Review,* 60 (1973), 393-405. This quote is from page 394.

25. Rousset, *Narcisse romancier,* pp. 21-22.

26. Spitzer, "Les*Lettres portugaises,*" *Romanische Forschungen* 65 (1954), 94-135.

27. I take the term, though not the meaning, from F. Jost's essay on epistolary fiction in his *Essais de littérature comparée.*

28. Richardson, *Pamela, or Virtue Rewarded,* ed. William M. Sale, Jr. (New York, 1958), p. 100. Another detailed example may be found on p. 45 of this edition.

29. For other aspects of the relationship between novels and manuals, see Bernard A. Bray, *L'Art de la lettre amoureuse: des manuels aux romans, 1550-1700* (The Hague, 1967). This is one of the best essays, some thirty pages long, on the subject. Manuals referred to in my discussion are: Pierre Ortique de Vaumorière, *Lettres sur toutes sortes de sujets, avec des avis sur la manière de les écrire* (Paris, 1699), and Eléazar de Mauvillon, *Traité général du Stile, avec un traité particulier du stile épistolaire* (Amsterdam, 1751).

30. Marivaux, *La Vie de Marianne,* ed. Deloffre (Paris, 1957), p. 9.

31. Stanley Fish, "Literature in the Reader: Affective Stylistics," *New Literary History* 2 (1970-71), 123-62, and other places.

32. Todorov, "Choderlos de Laclos et la théorie du récit," pp. 27, 28.

33. Richardson, "Preface to the *Familiar Letters,*" ed. Henley (New York, 1903), XVI, 20.

34. Braudy, "The Form of the Sentimental Novel," *Novel* 7 (1973), 6, 12, 13.

35. *Novel* 2 (1968), 5–14. Subsequent references to this piece will be found in the text.

Chapter Four

1. The most thorough bibliography of articles, notes, essays, monographs, etc. on the predecessors, adaptations, and interpretation of *Les Liaisons dangereuses* is to be found in Versini's enormous *Laclos et la tradition* (Paris, 1968), pp. 665–735.

2. Any critic of Laclos who has read Irving Wohlfarth's devastating critique is acutely aware of this possibility; see "The Irony of Criticism and the Criticism of Irony: A Study of Laclos Criticism," *Studies in Voltaire and the Eighteenth Century* 120 (1974), 269–317. The Laclos critics criticized by Wohlfarth are Rousset, Poulet, Todorov, and Daniel.

3. For a detailed account of some of these concerns, see Georges May's important study, *Le Dilemme du roman au dix-huitième siècle* (Paris, 1963).

4. See Todorov's *Littérature et signification* (Paris, 1967), pp. 39–49, another version of which appeared as "Choderlos de Laclos et la théorie du récit," *Tel Quel,* no. 27 (1966), pp. 7–12. See, as well, his "The Discovery of Language: *Les Liaisons dangereuses* and *Adolphe,*" *Yale French Studies* 45 (1970), 113–26. Henri Blanc's perceptive little study uses some of the same methodologies: *"Les Liaisons dangereuses" de Choderlos de Laclos* (Paris, 1972). See, as well, Janet Altman, "The 'Triple Register': Introduction to Temporal Complexity in the Letter-Novel," to appear in *L'Esprit Créateur,* vol. 17 (1978).

5. Rosbottom, "A Matter of Competence: The Relationship between Reading and Novel-making in Eighteenth-Century France," *Studies in Eighteenth-Century Culture* (Madison, Wis., 1977), VI, 245–63.

6. Barthes's most influential work in this field includes *S/Z* (Paris, 1970) and *Le Plaisir du texte* (Paris, 1973). Culler outlines a theory of reading in his *Structuralist Poetics* (London, 1975) which he applied in his *Flaubert* (Ithaca, 1974).

7. On the importance of what can be called a selective reading, see Barthes, *S/Z,* pp. 22–23, and p. 171. He states that "ceux qui négligent de relire s'obligent à lire partout la même histoire" ("Those who neglect to reread are forced to read everywhere the same story"). Henri Blanc, in his study of the *Liaisons,* develops a strategy (p. 19) for reading the correspondence similar to the one used in chapter 5 of this study: "une relecture monodique," i.e., reading only the letters of one or two correspondents, rather than the letters that accompany them as well.

8. Culler, *Flaubert: The Uses of Uncertainty,* pp. 14, 15.

9. Those who have read the attacks of the French philosopher Jacques

Derrida on "logocentrism" in Western metaphysics will recognize here an important theme in eighteenth-century French literature. See Derrida's extensive analysis of the philosophical implications of writing (*écriture*) in his *Of Grammatology* (Baltimore, 1976), especially pp. 95–316, which deal with Rousseau and Enlightenment theories of language.

10. Reference has already been made, in chapter 2, to the rearrangements that Laclos himself made in several sequences. See note 12 of chapter 2 as well as Seylaz, *"Les Liaisons dangereuses,"* pp. 31–33.

11. There are slight discrepancies in the placing of notes between the manuscript of the *Liaisons* and the first and subsequent editions of the novel. The total difference in these cases does not amount to more than a dozen additions or deletions. See Thelander, *Laclos and the Epistolary Novel*, p. 31, for a brief analysis of these emendations.

12. On this important aspect of Valmont's language, see especially Georges May's "The Witticisms of Monsieur de Valmont," *L'Esprit Créateur* 3 (1963), 181–87.

13. Culler, *Flaubert*, pp. 79–80. Culler's reading of Flaubert has obviously influenced and substantiated mine of Laclos. Though he sees Flaubert as forming a watershed in the history of narrative fiction in Europe, I would argue that novels such as *La Nouvelle Héloïse* and *Les Liaisons dangereuses* contain intimations of the same philosophical approach to the dangers of reading and writing that define Flaubert's *oeuvre*.

Chapter Five

1. Baudelaire, *Curiosités esthétiques,* ed. Lemaître (Paris, 1962), p. 832.

2. Jean-Luc Seylaz, in his *"Les Liaisons dangereuses" et la création romanesque chez Laclos* (Geneva, 1958), was among the first to draw attention to the special structural significance of this odd couple. He writes: "The master stroke ... was the invention of the Valmont-Merteuil couple" (p. 20). Earlier, he had stated more specifically that "the complicity which unites Mme de Merteuil and Valmont appears perilous from the beginning, and their friendship appears threatened. To be convinced of this, one has only to reread the first letters they exchange. They are striking by their tone of mockery, a mixture of teasing and violence" (p. 14).

Another excellent analysis of the Merteuil-Valmont relationship is Aram Vartanian's "The Marquise de Merteuil: A Case of Mistaken Identity," *L'Esprit Créateur* 3 (1963), 172–80.

3. Duranton, *"Les Liaisons dangereuses ou le miroir ennemi,"* *Revue des sciences humaines,* no. 153 (1974), pp. 125–43. Further references to this article will appear in the text.

4. See especially, on this point, D. A. Coward, "Laclos and the *Dénouement* of the *Liaisons dangereuses*," *Eighteenth-Century Studies* 5 (1972), 431–49, and Lloyd R. Free, "Crébillon *fils,* Laclos, and the Code of the Libertine," *Eighteenth-Century Life* 1 (1974), 36–40.

5. For purposes of the present study, I have condensed somewhat the arguments of this chapter. For a more detailed version of this essay, including an overview of systems theory and its use by the Palo Alto group, see my "Dangerous Connections: A Communicational Approach to *Les Liaisons dangereuses*," in *Laclos: Critical Approaches to "Les Liaisons dangereuses*," ed. Free (Madrid, 1978).

6. See his *Littérature et signification* (Paris, Larousse, 1967), "Les Catégories du récit littéraire," *Communications* 8 (1966), 125–51, and "Choderlos de Laclos et la théorie du récit," *Tewl Quel,* no. 27 (1966), pp. 17–28. In his article in *Communications,* Todorov suggests that "the study of character poses many problems which are still far from being resolved. We will consider a character type which is relatively well-studied: *the one defined completely by his relationships with other characters.* Even though the total meaning of each element in a work equals the combination of its relations with the other elements, one must not conclude that every personage is defined entirely by his relatinships with all the other personages. This is however the case for a type of literature [i.e., the epistolary novel] and most notably for the drama" (pp. 132–33, my italics).

7. Elsa First, "The New Wave in Psychiatry," *New York Review of Books* (20 February 1975), p. 8. This review article of recent publications of the "family therapists" is an excellent critical overview of the group's philosophical and practical underpinnings.

8. See especially his seminal article on the "double-bind" theory of schizophrenia written in 1956, and reprinted in a collection of his most important essays, *Steps to an Ecology of Mind* (New York, 1974), pp. 201–27.

9. Paul Watzlawick, John H. Weakland, Richard Fisch, *Change: Principles of Problem Formation and Problem Resolution* (New York, 1974), p. xiv.

10. Some readers will no doubt bring to mind here Roman Jakobson's famous outline of the functions of any speech event, where he asserts that every message requires "a *contact,* a physical channel and psychological connection between the addresser and the addressee, enabling both of them to enter and stay in communication." The linguistic function determined by this factor is the *phatic* one, which seeks "to establish, to prolong, or to discontinue communication, to check whether the channel works, to attract the attention of the interlocutor or to confirm his continued attention" ("Linguistics and Poetics," in *Style in Language,* ed. T. Sebeok [Cambridge, Mass., 1960], pp. 353, 355). Though my approach refers less to linguistic and more to psychological symptomata, the parallels between it and Jakobson's theory are manifest.

11. By Paul Watzlawick, Janet H. Beavin, Don D. Jackson (New York, 1967). Future references to this book will appear in the text.

12. In his fine article, "The Marquise de Merteuil: A Case of Mistaken Identity," Aram Vartanian recognizes such a situation when he writes about Merteuil that "her culminating blunder may be explained by assuming that, in her complicity with Valmont, there was some basic *malentendu* to which she remained blind and was consequently unable to include in her calculations" (p. 175).

13. In fact, Watzlawick's group applies their axioms, with successful results, to Edward Albee's play, *Who's Afraid of Virginia Wolf?*, pp. 149–86.

14. *Steps to an Ecology of Mind,* pp. 201–27.

15. See Watzlawick, et. al., pp. 108–9. For a fuller explanation of the concepts of "symmetrical escalation," "rigid complementarity," and of the definition of self in communicational exchange, see also, pp. 107–17 and 83–90, respectively.

16. Ruesch and Bateson, *Communication: The Social Matrix of Psychiatry* (New York, 1968), p. 179.

17. Ibid., p. 38.

Chapter Six

1. Baudelaire, *Curiosités esthétiques,* ed. Lemaître (Paris, 1962), p. 831. Further references to this edition will appear in the text.

2. Giraudoux, *Littérature* (Paris, 1941), p. 87. Further references to this essay will appear in the text.

3. Duranton, *"Les Liaisons dangereuses* ou le miroir ennemi," p. 127.

4. For instance, Caussy discusses, but finally rejects the suggestion that, while in prison, Laclos composed Vilate's *Des Causes secrètes de la révolution du 9 thermidor* (p. 280). Another example of this tendency to depict Laclos as amanuensis and of a modern scholar's investigation of it is D. A. Coward's article, "Laclos a-t-il participé aux *Galeries des Etats-Généraux?" Zeitschrift für Französische Sprache und Literatur* 84 (1974), 130–47. The answer, by the way, is no; Laclos had nothing to do with this satirical piece.

5. Daniel, *Fatalité du secret et fatalité du bavardage au XVIIIe siècle* (Paris, 1966). Further references to this essay will appear in the text.

Selected Bibliography

PRIMARY SOURCES

1. Complete Editions

The best available complete edition of Choderlos de Laclos's works in French is the one published in the Bibliothèque de la Pléiade series (Paris: Gallimard, 1943; 2d. ed. 1951). Edited with an introduction and notes by Maurice Allem, this edition contains:

Les Liaisons dangereuses (pp. 5–399).
De l'Education des femmes (pp. 403–58).
Poésies (pp. 461–95), including all known verse pieces by Laclos.
Critique littéraire (pp. 499–539), including "Sur le roman de: *Cecilia,*" "Le Voyage de La Pérouse."
Oeuvres politiques (pp. 569–654).

In the appendix (pp. 657–98) to this edition, Allem has placed works whose authorship had been attributed to Laclos but whose authenticity he believed to be still in question. However, since this edition, all of the political works have been confirmed as having been written by Laclos (see on this point, P.-E. Levayer, "Les Ecrits politiques de Laclos," *Revue d'histoire littéraire de France* 69 [1969], 51–60). These include the non-political "Projet de numérotage des rues et des maisons de Paris," as well as the *Instructions envoyées par le duc d'Orléans aux Assemblées des bailliages,* the *Exposé de la conduite de M. de duc d'Orléans dans la Révolution française,* and two portraits, "Elmire" and "Polixène," that appeared in the satirical *Galerie des Dames françaises,* and probably were *not* written by Laclos. Also, included in the appendix is the very important correspondence between Laclos and Madame Riccoboni about the *Liaisons* (pp. 686–98).

2. Correspondence with wife and poems.

Lettres inédites de Choderlos de Laclos. Edited by Louis de Chauvigny (Paris: Mercure de France, 1914).
Poésies de Choderlos de Laclos. Edited by Arthur Symons et Louis Thomas (Paris: Dorbon, 1908).

3. The commentary on Lacretelle's play has yet to be published under Laclos's name, but may be found as follows:

PICHOIS, CLAUDE. "Un roman méconnu et inachevé de Choderlos de Laclos." In *Saggi e ricerche di letteratura francese*. Milan: Feltrinelli, 1960. I, 87–148.

4. Separate Editions of *Les Liaisons dangereuses*

The most easily available of these editions, in French, besides Allem's edition, are, in chronological order:

Les Liaisons dangereuses. Edited by Edouard Maynial. 2 vols. Paris: Société d'Edition "Les Belles Lettres," 1943.

Les Liaisons dangereuses. Edited by Roger Vailland. Paris: Club français du livre, 1957; rpt. 1965.

Les Liaisons dangereuses. Edited by Yves Le Hir. Classiques Garnier. Paris: Garnier, 1961. This edition is the only available one which follows exactly the Bibliothèque Nationale copy of the *Liaisons* manuscript.

Les Liaisons dangereuses. Edited by René Pomeau. Paris: Garnier-Flammarion, 1964.

Les Liaisons dangereuses. Edited by Jean Mistler. Le Livre de Poche. Paris: Librairie Générale de France, 1972.

5. A Note on Translations

The only work of Laclos's that has been translated into English is *Les Liaisons dangereuses*. Fortunately, two of these translations are still in print:

Dangerous Acquaintances. Translated by Richard Aldington. New York: E. P. Dutton, 1924. Reprinted as *Liaisons Dangereuses*. New York: New American Library, 1962. As far as I know, this edition is still available.

Les Liaisons Dangereuses. Translated by P.W.K. Stone. Baltimore and Harmondsworth: Penguin Books, 1961. This is the edition I have used in the present study. It has just been reprinted.

SECONDARY SOURCES

1. Laclos and *Les Liaisons dangereuses*

There is no way in a short space to treat adequately the extensive Laclos bibliography. The most thorough bibliographic listing extant is in Versini's *Laclos et la tradition* (pp. 665–735). I have listed below those studies that have been most useful in the preparation of this book as well as those that are more easily accessible than others. Careful attention to the Notes and. References section of the present study will reveal other, more specialized titles.

BELAVAL, YVON. *Choderlos de Laclos.* Ecrivains d'hier et d'aujourd'hui, no. 40. Paris: Seghers, 1972. Perspicacious remarks on Laclos and his works; generous excerpts from the correspondence and from the *Liaisons.*

BLANC, HENRI. *"Les Liaisons dangereuses" de Choderlos de Laclos.* Poche critique. Paris: Hachette, 1972. A short (93 pp.) though excellent introduction to the dynamics of Laclos's novel. Uses persuasively some contemporary critical methodology.

BROOKS, PETER. *"Les Liaisons dangereuses."* In his *The Novel of Worldliness: Crébillon, Marivaux, Laclos, Stendhal.* Princeton: Princeton University Press, 1969, pp. 172-218. When read in conjunction with other essays in the book, this is one of the best introductions to Laclos's world view available.

CAUSSY, FERNAND. *Laclos, 1741-1803.* Paris: Mercure de France, 1905. With Dard's study, the only serious essay on Laclos's life. Not outdated.

DARD, ÉMILE. *Le Général Choderlos de Laclos, auteur des "Liaisons dangereuses": Un Acteur caché du drame révolutionnaire, 1741-1803.* Paris: Perrin, 1905. Title shows emphasis of this important biography.

DELMAS, ANDRÉ, and YVETTE. *A la recherche des "Liaisons dangereuses."* Paris: mercure de France, 1964. Best work available on Laclos's literary posterity and reputation.

DURANTON, HENRI. *"Les Liaisons dangereuses ou le miroir ennemi."* *Revue des sciences humaines,* no. 153 (1974), 125-43. Of dozens of recent articles on the *Liaisons,* this one ranks at the top. An intelligent appraisal of libertinism.

GIRAUDOUX, JEAN. "Choderlos de Laclos." In his *Littérature.* Paris: (1963), 47-53. Uses a careful reading of *De l'Éducation des femmes* to write an excellent article on Laclos and the condition of women in the eighteenth century.
Laclos's political writings; especially important on their authenticity.

HOFFMAN, PAUL. "Aspects de la condition féminine dans *Les Liaisons dangereuses* de Choderlos de Laclos." *L'Information littéraire* 15 (1963), 47-53. Uses a careful reading of *De l'éducation des femmes* to write an excellent article on Laclos and the condition of women in the eighteenth century.

LEVAYER, PAUL-ÉDOUARD. "Les Ecrits politiques de Laclos." *Revue d'histoire littéraire de France* 69 (1969), 51-60. A useful overview of Laclos's political writings, especially important on their authenticity.

MALRAUX, ANDRÉ. "Laclos et *Les Liaisons dangereuses,*" in his *Le Triangle noir: Laclos, Goya, Saint-Just.* Paris: Gallimard, 1970, pp. 23-51. First published in 1939, and often reprinted, this is an analysis of the "mythology of intelligence" created by merteuil and Valmont.

MILLER, NANCY K. "Female Sexuality and Narrative Structure in *La Nouvelle Héloïse* and *Les Liaisons dangereuses*." *Signs* 1 (1976), 609–38. A clear and pertinent treatment of women in Laclos's novel; especially good on Tourvel.

PIZZORUSSO, ARNALDO. "La struttura delle *Liaisons dangereuses*." In his *Studi sulla letteratura dell'età preromantica in Francia*. Pisa: Goliardica, 1956, pp. 7–52. A very good analysis of the structure of the *Liaisons*; also, of the place of the novel within Laclos's *oeuvre*, as well as its relationship with French fiction of the period. Extensive notes.

POMEAU, RENÉ. *Laclos*. Connaissance des Lettres. Paris: Haiter, 1975. The culmination of years of work on Laclos; short, to the point; a good introduction.

POULET, GEORGES. "Chamfort and Laclos." In his *The Interior Distance*. Baltimore: Johns Hopkins University Press, 1959. Pp. 45–64. An important treatment of Laclos's use of fictional time; should be read in the context of Poulet's other works on time.

RAAPHORST, MADELEINE. "Choderlos de Laclos et l'éducation des femmes au 18e siècle." *Rice University Studies* 53 (1967), 33–41. Useful survey of Laclos's essays.

SEYLAZ, JEAN-LUC. *"Les Liaisons dangereuses" et la création romanesque chez Laclos*. Geneva: Droz, 1958. Without question, the best book on Laclos's novel as a fictional construct.

THELANDER, DOROTHY. *Laclos and the Epistolary Novel*. Geneva: Droz, 1963. The most thorough book-length study on Laclos's epistolary format.

THODY, PHILLIP. *Laclos: "Les Liaisons dangereuses."* Studies in French Literature, no. 14. London: Arnold, 1970. A short (63 pp.) and well-written introduction to the *Liaisons*. In English.

TODOROV, TZVETAN. *Littérature et signification*. Paris: Larousse, 1967. An important structuralist reading of the *Liaisons*, emphasizing the work's self-consciousness.

TURNELL, MARTIN. "Choderlos de Laclos and *Les Liaisons dangereuses*." In his *The Novel in France: Mme. de La Fayette, Laclos, Constant, Stendhal, Balzac, Flaubert, Proust*. New York: Vintage Books, 1951. Pp. 49–79. Very readable, at times infuriatingly moralistic interpretation of the *Liaisons*. Important essay that introduced novel to English-speaking readers.

VAILLAND, ROGER. *Laclos par lui-même*. Ecrivains de Toujours. Paris: Seuil, 1953. A sensitive Marxist approach to the *Liaisons*, with many excerpts from the novel, as well as iconographical material.

VARTANIAN, ARAM. "The Marquise de Merteuil: A Case of Mistaken Identity." *L'Esprit Créateur* 3 (1963), 172–80. Its title does not do justice to this richly imaginative analysis of eroticism and the Merteuil-Valmont relationship.

VERSINI, LAURENT. *Laclos et la tradition: Essai sur les sources et la tech-*

nique des "Liaisons dangereuses." Paris: Klincksieck, 1968. An enormous (793 pages) compendium of every work or tradition that might have influenced Laclos or have been influenced by him. Very useful, almost definitive bibliography.

2. Background and Other Critical Studies

ALTMAN, JANET. "Epistolarity: Approaches to a Form." Ph.D. Diss. Yale, 1973. The most comprehensive and convincing analysis of this narrative subgenre available.

BARTHES, ROLAND. *S/Z.* Translated by R. Howard. New York: Hill and Wang, 1974. An important book that raises questions about how we read fictional texts.

COULET, HENRI. *Le Roman jusqu'à la Révolution.* Paris: Armand Colin, 1967. The best introduction to French fiction before 1800.

CULLER, JONATHAN. *Flaubert: The Uses of Uncertainty.* Ithaca: Cornell University Press, 1974. A study that goes beyond its subject to examine the premises of narrative fiction in France before as well as after Flaubert.

DARNTON, ROBERT. "Reading, Writing, and Publishing in Eighteenth-Century France: A Case Study in the Sociology of Literature." *Daedalus,* no. 100 (Winter 1971), pp. 214–56. Required reading for those who want to know the ins and outs of book-publishing during the Enlightenment in France.

MAY, GEORGES. *Le Dilemme du roman au XVIIIe siècle: Etude sur les rapports du roman et de la critique (1715–1761).* Paris: Presses Universitaires de France, 1963. Influential study on the question of fiction's morality and how debate on the subject affected the novel's development.

MYLNE, VIVIENNE. *The Eighteenth-Century French Novel: Techniques of Illusion.* Manchester: Manchester University Press, 1965. Useful introduction to French novel during this period. Includes essays on Lesage, Prévost, Marivaux, Diderot, Rousseau, and Laclos (pp. 233–44).

ROUSSET, JEAN. *Narcisse romancier: Essai sur la première personne dans le roman.* Paris: Corti, 1973. Very well-written essays on first-person narration and its thematic use.

————. "Une Forme littéraire: Le roman par lettres." In his *Forme et signification: Essais sur les structures littéraires de Corneille à Claudel.* Paris: Corti, 1974. Pp. 65–108. Concise introduction to techniques of epistolary fiction.

SHOWALTER, ENGLISH. *The Evolution of the French Novel, 1641–1782.* Princeton: Princeton University Press, 1972. An essential history of French fiction, with perspicacious pages on Laclos.

STEWART, PHILLIP. *Imitation and Illusion in the French Memoir-Novel, 1700–1750. The Art of Make-Believe.* New Haven: Yale University

Press, 1969. A very good overview of the other major first-person, fictional subgenre of the eighteenth century.

_____. *Le Masque et la parole: Le langage de l'amour au XVIIIe siècle.* Paris: Corti, 1973. An attempt at analyzing, on a thematic level, the special "language of love" of eighteenth-century fiction; includes a short essay on the *Liaisons* (pp. 185–95).

Index

163